THE ENCYCLOPEDIA OF
CONTEMPORARY
JEWELLERY MAKING
TECHNIQUES

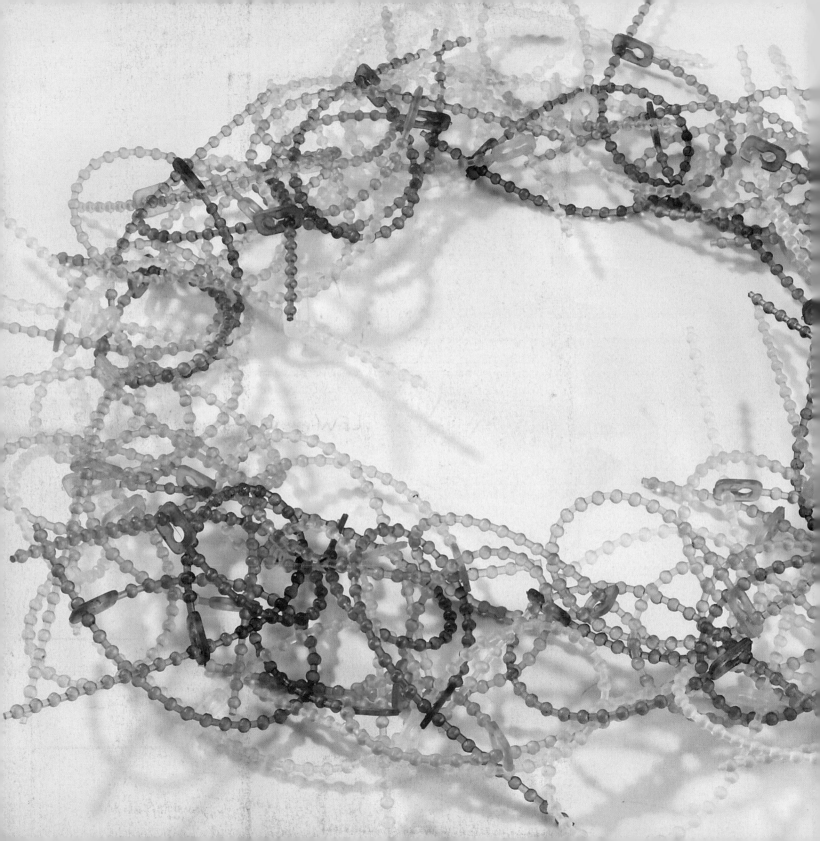

THE ENCYCLOPEDIA OF
CONTEMPORARY
JEWELLERY MAKING
TECHNIQUES

VANNETTA SEECHARRAN

Search Press

A QUARTO BOOK

Published in 2009 by Search Press Ltd
Wellwood
North Farm Road
Tunbridge Wells
Kent TN2 3DR

Reprinted 2010

ISBN 978-1-84448-490-4

QUAR.CJT

Conceived, designed and produced by
Quarto Publishing plc
The Old Brewery
6 Blundell Street
London N7 9BH

Additional text by Joanne Haywood

SENIOR EDITOR: Lindsay Kaubi
COPY EDITOR: Liz Dalby
ART DIRECTOR: Caroline Guest
ART EDITORS: Anna Plucinska and
    Jacqueline Palmer
DESIGNER: Elizabeth Healey
PHOTOGRAPHER: Simon Pask
PICTURE RESEARCHER: Sarah Bell
CREATIVE DIRECTOR: Moira Clinch
PUBLISHER: Paul Carslake

Colour separation by PICA Digital Pte Ltd,
Singapore
Printed in China by 1010 Printing International

10 9 8 7 6 5 4 3 2 1

CONTENTS

INTRODUCTION

Traditionally jewellery has been made from metal, and although that is still the case, in recent years jewellery makers have increasingly turned to non-traditional materials for their work. Contemporary jewellers make use of a vast range of materials, and combinations of many materials can sometimes be seen in just a single piece of jewellery.

The aim of this book is to inspire students, professional jewellers and anyone with an interest in making jewellery to experiment with materials. It's a common misconception that jewellery should be made with precious materials, but it is not the material that makes jewellery precious, it is ideas and the creative use of materials. This book aims to inspire people to investigate non-precious materials and to explore their almost limitless possibilities for jewellery making.

This book is divided into six chapters, organized by material. Each chapter includes step-by-step guides to working with each material in interesting and unexpected ways. The techniques described should enable you to experiment and develop new and exciting methods of working to create interesting and innovative pieces of jewellery.

More traditional jewellery-making techniques, such as working with metal: soldering, shaping, piercing and polishing are included, while weaving, crocheting and knotting are borrowed from textiles, and other techniques are introduced

CROCHET NECKLACE
by Karla Schabert
Cotton thread crocheted around glass beads.

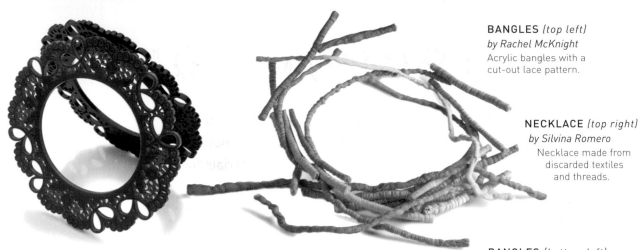

BANGLES *(top left)*
by Rachel McKnight
Acrylic bangles with a
cut-out lace pattern.

NECKLACE *(top right)*
by Silvina Romero
Necklace made from
discarded textiles
and threads.

from many disciplines, including plastics, woodwork, glass, ceramics, paper and even concrete. There are also fascinating examples of finished jewellery pieces to inspire design ideas and a description of the stages of the jewellery-making process.

This book will introduce you to the vast range of materials and media being used by jewellers today, and show examples of inspiring work by leading contemporary jewellers. You will learn the basic skills needed to work with the materials covered in the book, and will be inspired to experiment and develop your own techniques and create your own contemporary jewellery.

BANGLES *(bottom left)*
by Lesley Strickland
These heat-formed bangles are made
from a plastic called cellulose acetate.

RINGS *(bottom centre left)*
by Vannetta Seecharran
Rings made from heat-formed plastic.

NECKPIECE *(bottom centre right)*
by Min-Ji Cho
Neckpiece made from rubber gloves,
sterling silver and freshwater pearls.

CHAIN *(bottom right)*
by Joanne Haywood
Neck chain made with textiles and
oxidized silver.

TOOLS

THERE ARE A HUGE RANGE OF JEWELLERY TOOLS AVAILABLE, AND YOU WILL NEED TO BUILD YOUR COLLECTION OVER TIME. WHEN BUYING TOOLS FOR JEWELLERY MAKING YOU SHOULD BUY THE BEST YOU CAN AFFORD.

SOLDERING TOOLS

Soldering is a way of connecting pieces of metal together. Before soldering can begin, some preparation is required. Choose a surface that is free of any flammable materials in a space that is well ventilated. Be sure that you have the appropriate dish for the pickle solution and soldering tools.

SOLDERING BLOCKS AND TORCH

Before setting up to solder it is important to have the correct soldering block and torch. Use a large soldering mat to protect the work surface and a smaller block for soldering. Choose the correct size and type of torch. This torch is ideal for small pieces such as rings and earrings.

PICKLE CONTAINER

Store pickle solution in a toughened glass container that has a secure lid. Keep the container closed when you are not using the solution. Use only copper or brass tongs or tweezers to remove pieces from the pickle solution. Steel tweezers will contaminate the pickle and copper-plate any silver pieces already in the container.

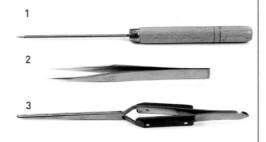

1 PROBE

During soldering the solder chips may move away from the seam – use a probe to push them back into place.

2 STEEL TWEEZERS

These steel tweezers have a very sharp tip and are used to place solder chips in position to be soldered.

3 INSULATED CROSS-LOCKING TWEEZERS

Cross-locking tweezers open when you squeeze the handle. They are used to hold small pieces for soldering.

MEASURING AND MARKING TOOLS

Measuring tools are important in jewellery making, for measuring and cutting metal pieces accurately.

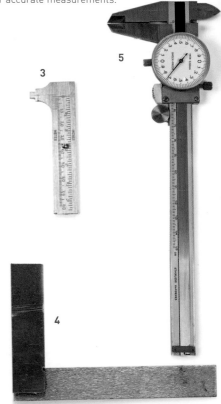

1 DIVIDER

Circles can be drawn with a divider.

2 RULER

A 15-cm (6-in) metal ruler is useful for drawing straight lines.

3 BRASS CALIPER

A caliper is used for measuring.

4 STEEL RIGHT ANGLE

This tool is used to mark out perfect right angles.

5 LARGE CALIPER

One end of the caliper is used for measuring the inside diameter of a shape and the other is used for measuring the outside. The dial allows for accurate measurements.

SHAPING TOOLS

Metal can be stretched, shaped and manipulated in many different ways. Before shaping a sheet of metal, it should be annealed to make it more malleable. However, while it is being shaped it will work-harden and need annealing; several annealings may be necessary, depending on the desired shape. Sheets can be hammered over shaping tools such as stakes and mandrels or into a doming block to create spheres.

1 ROUND RING MANDREL
A soldered ring is placed over the mandrel and hammered until round with a rawhide mallet.

2 OVAL MANDREL
An oval mandrel is used to make oval shapes by hammering with a rawhide mallet.

3 ROUND JUMP-RING MANDREL
Very small soldered rings can be shaped by placing them inside the mandrel and hammering them round.

4 SQUARE MANDREL
Square shapes can be made by hammering around a square mandrel.

5 CHASING HAMMER
A chasing hammer is used to hammer the head of a chasing punch. Chasing punches have different shaped ends for stamping out decorative designs on sheet metal.

6 EMBOSSING HAMMER
Hammering a sheet of metal with an embossing hammer stretches and hardens the surface and creates a rounded, indented texture.

7 BALL-PEEN HAMMER
A ball-peen hammer's rounded head works metal smoothly without marking it. The ball portion can straighten and stretch metal into the desired shape.

8 RAWHIDE MALLET
Rawhide mallets are made from buffalo rawhide and are secured on a wooden handle. They are used for shaping sheet metal.

9 WOODEN BOSSING MALLET
Soft sheet metal, such as lead, can be shaped with a wooden bossing hammer.

10 NYLON CROSS-PEEN MALLET
The narrowing at one end of a cross-peen mallet is used for shaping sheet metal without marking the surface.

11 RIVETING HAMMER
A riveting hammer is used for hammering the end of a wire to make a rivet.

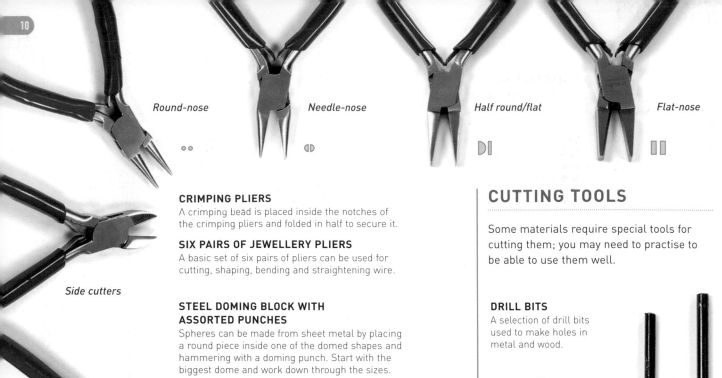

Round-nose   Needle-nose   Half round/flat   Flat-nose

Side cutters

End cutters

Crimping pliers

CRIMPING PLIERS

A crimping bead is placed inside the notches of the crimping pliers and folded in half to secure it.

SIX PAIRS OF JEWELLERY PLIERS

A basic set of six pairs of pliers can be used for cutting, shaping, bending and straightening wire.

STEEL DOMING BLOCK WITH ASSORTED PUNCHES

Spheres can be made from sheet metal by placing a round piece inside one of the domed shapes and hammering with a doming punch. Start with the biggest dome and work down through the sizes.

STEEL STAKES

Sheet metal can be shaped by hammering it over a stake with a metal hammer or rawhide mallet.

CUTTING TOOLS

Some materials require special tools for cutting them; you may need to practise to be able to use them well.

DRILL BITS

A selection of drill bits used to make holes in metal and wood.

GLASS CUTTER

A cutter with a special tip for cutting through glass. Oil fills the cavity of the handle and lubricates the blade during cutting.

1 LARGE FLAT FILE
Large files are flat on the front and back and the sides are parallel. They are available in many cut sizes and are used for filing metal.

2 LARGE HALF-ROUND FILE
A half-round file has a flat side and a curved side and is tapered towards the tip. The round side is used for filing inside curved shapes.

3 LARGE BARRETTE FILE
A barrette file has teeth on just one side and is used for filing flat surfaces.

4 SHAPED FILES
The ends of these files are completely round and are ideal for filing hard-to-reach areas.

5 NEEDLE FILES
Needle files are small files and are available in many different shapes such as square, round and triangular.

METAL BURRS
A selection of metal burrs. These have many purposes, from grinding unwanted solder to carving metal for stone setting.

SHEARS
Simple shapes can be cut out of thin sheet metal with shears.

JEWELLERY SAW
A jewellery saw is essential for piercing more complex shapes from sheet metal.

SAW BLADES
Blades for a jewellery saw are very fine and can cut through a range of thicknesses of metal.

1 LEATHER KNIFE

The strong blade of this knife is ideal for cutting leather.

2 SKIVING KNIFE

A skiving knife is used for thinning leather; for example, seams may need to be made thinner to allow for smooth joins.

1 HOLE PUNCHES

Punches are used for making holes in leather. Should be used on a cutting mat.

2 EYELET PUNCH

An eyelet is placed in the punch and the ends are spread to secure

WAX-CARVING TOOLS

These tools are made especially for carving hard wax suitable for jewellery making. The tips of the tools can be heated for easier carving. Carving files have coarse teeth and are used for initially shaping the wax.

1 RING SIZER

This wooden tool has a flat side with a metal strip, and one edge of the strip is a sharp blade that can cut through the wax. The tool is placed inside a piece of wax and twisted to correct the size of a mould.

2 HALF-ROUND WAX FILE

Wax files have very coarse teeth and are used for shaping and carving wax.

3 NEEDLE FILES

Wax needle files have coarse teeth to cut through carving wax.

4 WAX-CARVING TOOLS

Carving tools are metal tools that can be used hot to carve wax. The tip of each tool is different to carve a range of shapes.

POLISHING AND FINISHING TOOLS

Metal can be finished with a polishing motor. A variety of wheels can be used to achieve either a highly polished or a textured finish. Hand polishing can be done with a selection of wet and dry sandpaper and a brass or steel brush.

POLISHING MOTOR

A polishing motor has a horizontal shaft on which polishing wheels can be mounted for different polishing jobs

RING POLISHING WHEELS

1 Buffing wheel.
2 Fine wheel – to sand the inside of a ring.
3 Final polishing wheel.

BRUSHES

1 A steel brush is used for cleaning files and can also be used on metal for a textured finish.
2 A useful brush to use for cleaning and finishing metal.

1 CENTRE PUNCH

A centre punch is used for marking metal before drilling so that the drill bit is guided into the correct position.

2 SCRIBER

A scriber is a marking tool used for drawing designs on metal in preparation for piercing.

ATTACHMENTS FOR A FLEXSHAFT MOTOR

1 Polishing wheel.
2 Grinding wheel for removing lots of material very quickly.
3 Sanding disk.

WHEELS FOR USE ON A POLISHING MOTOR

1 Scotchbrite wheel – gives a beautiful satin finish to metal.
2 Coarse grinding wheel – will remove excessive material very quickly and is ideal for removing sprues after casting
3 Polishing wheel.
4 Fabric wheel used for achieving a high polish on metal.

SANDING DISCS (BELOW)

Assorted sanding and grinding discs can be used with a flexshaft motor (left). These discs are useful for sanding hard-to-reach areas such as corners.

MISCELLANEOUS TOOLS

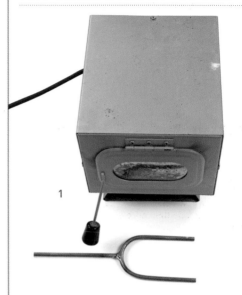

1 KILN

A kiln can be used for enamelling and for fusing glass sheets together.

2 BENCH PEG WITH ANVIL

A portable bench peg anvil has a wooden peg with a V-shaped cut-out and a metal surface that can be used for hammering. It can be clamped to any sturdy bench for piercing and hammering metal.

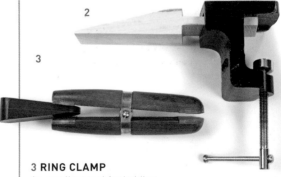

3 RING CLAMP

An excellent tool for holding small pieces for filing or stone setting, for example.

DESIGNING CONTEMPORARY JEWELLERY

CONTEMPORARY JEWELLERY DESIGN OPENS UP AN IMMENSE CHOICE OF MATERIALS TO WORK WITH. SOMETIMES TWO OR THREE MATERIALS WILL BE USED TOGETHER IN ONE DESIGN. MATERIALS SUCH AS PLASTIC, GLASS, FABRICS, FOUND OBJECTS AND PAPER ALL HAVE DIFFERENT PROPERTIES, BOTH VISUALLY AND PHYSICALLY. THESE PROPERTIES NEED TO BE TAKEN INTO CONSIDERATION WHEN THINKING ABOUT DESIGN.

Methods of designing contemporary jewellery can vary as much as the materials you choose to work with. However, the following areas will probably feature in most designers' work.

USING A VISUAL JOURNAL

A visual journal is normally the starting point and involves collecting materials from any visual source that you find interesting and thought-provoking. This can take the form of your own drawings from primary sources, photographs, illustrations, found objects, or anything that you are drawn to. Over time you will probably find that you begin to see a connection between many of the sources. For example, choosing to look at colour in a particular way, repeated patterns, mutation in nature, museum artefacts, narratives and theories. Your own observational drawings are a good starting point and through developing, observing and recording you will develop your design skills. Visual journals should also include your own notation. For example, if you are looking at a museum artefact you would record the date, title, materials, catalogue numbers and anything else that may be important to remember.

DESIGN BOOK

From your initial visual research, you then move on to working in a design book, recording initial ideas, developing a concept (your ideas and intentions) and designing what to make. You should take into account the materials, scale, colour, techniques and processes as well as the type of object you wish to design, e.g. brooch, chain or ring. Once you have your designs, you can experiment with your ideas as a series of test pieces before progressing on to prototypes and a final piece. Throughout this process you will find yourself returning

VISUAL RESEARCH
by Loukia Richards
These initial sketches of seventeenth-century Greek embroidery from the Textile Museum's collection, Washington, DC (above), show the development from initial textiles studies into a final fibre necklace (left).

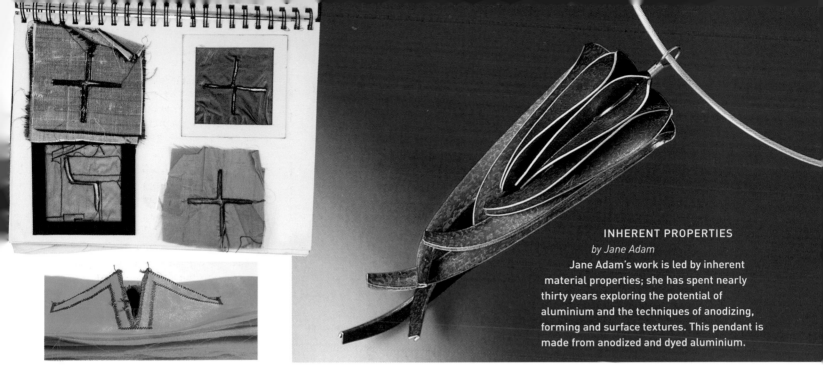

TEST PIECES FOR A FABRIC BRACELET
by Vannetta Seecharran
The test pieces for this fabric bracelet (above top) develop into a final piece (above bottom).

INHERENT PROPERTIES
by Jane Adam
Jane Adam's work is led by inherent material properties; she has spent nearly thirty years exploring the potential of aluminium and the techniques of anodizing, forming and surface textures. This pendant is made from anodized and dyed aluminium.

MULTIMEDIA
by Natalya Pinchuk
This mixed-media necklace demonstrates a careful balance of multiple materials: wool, copper, enamel, plastic, waxed thread, stainless steel.

to your sketch book to think through certain aspects of your designs and record any changes.

Models and test pieces are an essential part of designing, especially when you are exploring a new material, because you can't always foresee what will happen. By experimenting you can often uncover exciting results. Equally it allows you to work through any technical aspect that needs resolving, such as if a fastening on a bracelet will be able to keep the work securely on a wrist.

TECHNICAL JOURNAL
A technical journal is also a valuable tool when designing and making. It is used to record information on techniques and

TECHNICAL JOURNAL
by Elizabeth Olver
Before fabrication, pieces can be mapped out in a technical journal to check details and proportions.

processes as a reference for future works. It is important to record details about the price of materials and where you bought them, as well as step-by-step instructions on how the work was made, in order to

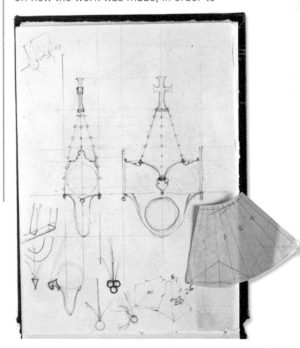

remake it. Quite often makers will record information visually by photographing work at its different stages.

Sometimes a visual journal, design book and/or technical journal will all be included in one book; however, it is often easier to separate them into three because it focuses your thoughts on each stage of the design process. Very often when you are making a new work there is a temptation to finish it as quickly as possible due to the excitement of seeing it completed. However, if you are patient and work through the cycle of designing and testing you will end up with more satisfying results.

INDIVIDUAL CHARACTER

Creating a strong identity in contemporary jewellery is something makers consider when designing. With an endless choice of materials and techniques it is possible with time and perseverance to develop work that has an individual character, easily recognizable as your own.

Many contemporary jewellers will design objects as a series. For example, you often find a series of rings that are subtly different; each one might vary in scale, colour and material but they will all connect together as a family of objects. This variation in design is less likely to occur in design work that is mass-produced. Making by hand is often a strong feature in contemporary jewellery.

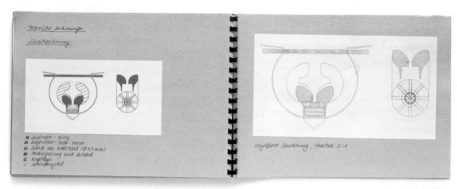

TECHNICAL DRAWING
by Jennifer Saners
The making of a piece can be recorded with technical drawings and photographs, as well as detailed text.

SCREEN-PRINTED NECKLACE
by Uli Rapp
Computer-aided design is now a popular method of designing. Uli Rapp designs her screen-printed jewellery with Adobe Illustrator. Her drawings can be taken directly from the computer to print on final pieces. This necklace is made from textiles, rubber and metal foil.

CHOOSING MATERIALS

When selecting materials to design with, there are no fixed rules as to whether the material should dictate what you make or the designs themselves shape the material you work in; either can be the case. Sometimes a jeweller will design a one-off piece where the choice of material is based on its symbolic meaning rather than its physical attributes. Other makers select materials because they are fascinated with their inherent properties. In this instance it is exciting to see how the work develops over time, with subtle changes and variations, ever growing and evolving.

Some makers like to design everything with paper and pencil thinking through every possibility before they touch materials. Nevertheless, when designing with fairly inexpensive materials such as paper, plastics and fabric, it is possible to design through a series of test pieces towards a final object. These test pieces can be seen as three-dimensional designing. At first it may seem strange to be making work without drawing every detail first. However, you are designing directly with the properties of the materials and many contemporary makers favour this design method.

Colour is an important factor when designing with materials such as fibres, plastic and glass. There is such a vast choice that colour often becomes a strong part of the concept.

Many materials chosen for contemporary jewellery impose their properties on jewellery design. For example, some materials cannot be heated without melting or being destroyed. In these instances other connections are employed, such as riveting, stapling and the use of adhesives. At a first glance, this may be considered a hindrance, but on the contrary, these conundrums can be an enjoyable part of designing.

The weight of a material often plays a role in designing. Plastics, rubber and textiles are comparably lightweight materials and therefore are suitable for large-scale work.

Material exploration in jewellery is not a modern trend. Hair, glass, fossilized wood, feathers and paper among many other materials have been used by our ancestors for thousands of years to make jewellery. Perhaps we now select and design with different motivations, but the desire to make and wear jewellery will always be with us.

COLOUR
by Ramon Puig Cuyàs
A maker for whom colour is a fundamental part of his designs is Spanish jeweller Ramon Puig Cuyàs. His spontaneous collaged works could only be produced in his materials: found plastics, glass, pebbles, metal, paint and wood. Trying to re-create these works in silver alone would have a completely different visual language.

RIVETS
by Hu Jun
Hu Jun, a Chinese jeweller, uses traditional lacquer work, which has to be cold connected in his work. The rivets are an intrinsic part of the design and not just included for their function.

MATERIAL QUALITIES
by Zoe Robertson
If Zoe Robertson's flocked acrylic and steel piece was made in a heavier material, such as solid spheres of gold, apart from being ludicrously expensive, it would be too heavy to wear.

CHAPTER 1

METAL
AND WIRE

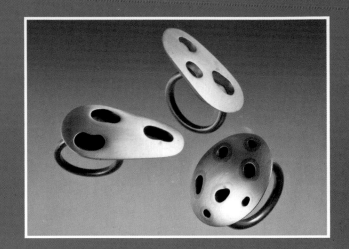

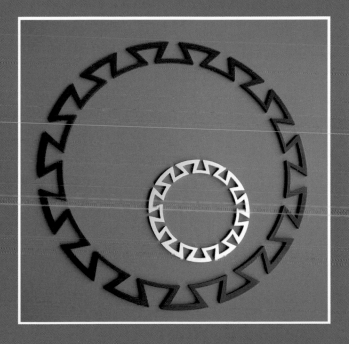

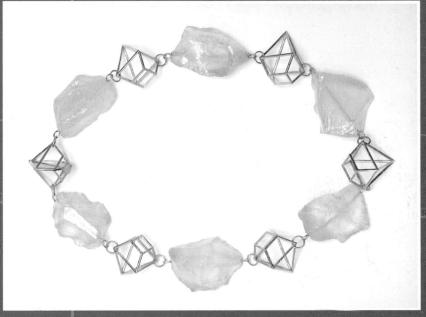

In this chapter, essential metal jewellery-making techniques, such as piercing, shaping and soldering, are described step by step to give you an introduction to working in metal. Through experimentation and practice you will develop your ideas and discover new methods of working.

BROOCH *(opposite)*
by Joanna Gollberg
Silver brooch with
semi-precious stones.

THREE RINGS *(top right)*
by Catherine Hills
Rings made from silver
and 18-carat gold.

BRACELET AND NECKLACE
(centre left)
by Fritz Maierhofer
Both bracelet and necklace are
made from eroded and
anodized aluminium.

NECKLACE *(centre right)*
by Philip Sajet
Necklace made from gold
wire and rose quartz.

METAL AND WIRE PROPERTIES

METAL IS A VERSATILE MATERIAL THAT HAS MANY APPLICATIONS, FROM MAKING JEWELLERY TO BEING USED IN INDUSTRY. BOTH PRECIOUS METALS SUCH AS GOLD AND SILVER AND BASE METALS SUCH AS COPPER AND BRASS CAN BE MANIPULATED THROUGH MELTING, HAMMERING AND FORMING AND CAN EVEN BE RECYCLED AND MADE INTO NEW PIECES. METAL IS AVAILABLE IN SHEET AND WIRE FORM FROM SPECIALIST JEWELLERY SUPPLIERS.

There are two main categories of metal: precious and base. The main precious metals are gold and silver, while the base category is wide and includes, copper, brass and steel.

Pure silver is a soft material and doesn't have the strength needed for making jewellery. To overcome this problem it is mixed with copper to form an alloy. 'Sterling silver' is an alloy made up of 92.5 per cent silver and 7.5 per cent copper and is stamped with the marking '925'. 'Fine silver' is 100 per cent pure silver, but its softness has advantages, and it can be used for enamelling and making bezel settings.

TUBING

WIRE

Like silver, gold can be alloyed with many different metals, and the 'carat' of gold is a measure of the proportion of gold in the alloy by weight, where 24c is pure and 18c is 75 per cent pure. The remainder of the alloy is a combination of copper, zinc and palladium to give the required strength and colour. 'White' gold is an alloy of gold and palladium.

Precious metals are available as sheets, wires, tubes and findings and are sold either by weight or by size. 'Findings' are individual components used as attachments in joining or linking pieces together. Examples include earring hooks, clasps and jump rings. Sheets of metal can be cut, hammered, stamped or textured and can be melted and reused.

Base metals are available in sheet, rod, wire, tube, foil and mesh products and are reasonably priced compared to precious metals. Base metal jewellery is often gold or silver plated to disguise the underlying metal and help keep costs down.

The range of tools available for working in metal is extensive and includes hammers, files, measuring tools, polishing motors and drills.

SHEETS

RODS AND SHAPED WIRE

DESIGNING WITH METAL AND WIRE

Quality Shiny, structured yet malleable, versatile, durable.

Applications Metal can be used for casting and sheets can be stretched and shaped for making silverware and jewellery. Pieces can be fused together, patterns can be applied to the surface and different colours can be combined to create effective patterns. Sheets can be made as thin as paper and manipulated by hand. Thick pieces can be carved and precious stones set into its surface.

Combining with other materials Metal can be combined with most materials, including plastic, fabric and leather. It is especially attractive when combined with plastic; contrasting the colourful qualities of plastic and the monotone surface of metal.

Where to look for inspiration Take a look at the websites below for inspiration from jewellers working with metal and wire.
- **Susan Skoczen, United States**
www.susanskoczen.com
Jewellery in precious metals with altered surfaces, using flocking, burnt paint and enamel.
- **Jane Adam, United Kingdom**
www.janeadam.com
Anodized aluminium jewellery, exploring colour, texture and surface.
- **Fabrizio Tridenti, Italy**
www.fabriziotridenti.it
Mixed-metal works with constantly evolving techniques and processes.

CUTTING AND PIERCING METAL

CUTTING METAL IS AN ESSENTIAL JEWELLERY TECHNIQUE AND ONCE PERFECTED IT CAN BE A FUN AND SATISFYING PROCESS. CUTTING AND PIERCING TECHNIQUES APPLY TO ALL METALS FROM GOLD TO COPPER, AND THE POSSIBILITIES ARE ENDLESS FOR CREATING BEAUTIFUL DESIGNS. IT'S A SIMPLE PROCESS THAT IS EASILY LEARNED.

TOOLS AND MATERIALS

SHEET METAL (IN THIS CASE SILVER)

SANDPAPER

SCRIBER

TRACING PAPER

PENCIL

SAW BLADES

SAW FRAME

BENCH PIN

DRILL

DRILL BIT

Learning how to use a jeweller's saw is one of the most important and basic skills in jewellery making. There are two basic types of saws: fixed and adjustable. A fixed saw has a frame that cannot be adjusted, but an adjustable saw allows you to use blades of varying lengths. There are a number of variations of the basic saw, and the depth of the saw frame can be anywhere from 5cm (2in) to 30cm (12in). Larger saw frames are used for cutting large pieces but are less stable and can be awkward to use. The standard frame size for cutting jewellery pieces is 7.5–10cm (3–4in).

Blades are sold in different sizes, and using the wrong blade can make cutting difficult and frustrating. Jewellery blades are very fine and range from size 8/0 (finest) to 8 (coarsest). Choosing the correct blade is important; as a rough guide, the correct blade has three teeth to the thickness of the metal. In general, choose a size 1 blade for 0.8–1mm (18–20 gauge) metal and a size 2 blade for 1–1.2mm (16–18 gauge). Blades are sold in packs of twelve individual blades or by the gross (which is twelve packs), and your supplier should be able to advise on the correct size. As a beginner you may use an entire pack cutting one piece so it's best to buy a few packs if you are cutting for the first time.

The cutting technique is the same for all metals. Copper and brass are great to use for practice; you can move on to precious metals once you feel comfortable with the technique.

MISMATCHED EARRINGS
by Marianne Anderson
These intricate earrings are created from similar but not identical pieces of pierced oxidized silver, suspended from freshwater pearls.

PIERCED PIECES
The finished pieces represent both the positive and negative shapes produced by piercing out shapes, and both could be used in jewellery pieces.

CUTTING OUT A DESIGN

1 PREPARING THE METAL

Before transferring your design to the metal, use a fine-grade sandpaper to sand the surface so it has a slight texture. This will allow you to transfer your design more easily and make it more visible when cutting.

2 SCRIBING THE DESIGN

Draw your design directly onto the metal with a scriber or draw it on a piece of tracing paper and trace over it with a scriber onto the metal. The scriber will cut through the paper and mark the metal.

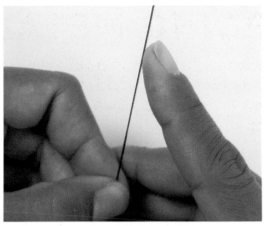

3 FINDING THE DIRECTION OF THE BLADE

Find the direction of the blade by rubbing your finger along the blade – it will snag on the direction of the teeth. The teeth of the blade should face up and point towards the handle of the saw frame.

4 INSERTING THE BLADE

Balance the saw between your body and the bench to free both of your hands. If you have an adjustable saw, the blade should be just short of the width of the saw frame. Insert the blade in the top end of the saw and tighten between the clamps on the saw frame.

Tip

Relax the hand holding the saw and don't push forwards with the blade. Pushing forwards will put too much tension on the blade and break it. Allow the saw to move freely up and down; it may be slow starting but will get faster in time.

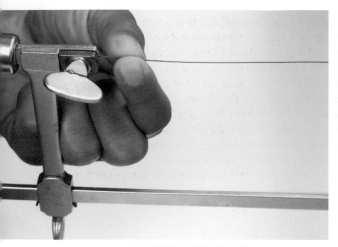

5 SECURING THE BLADE

Push the handle of the saw frame with your body to create tension in the frame. Insert the bottom end of the blade in the saw frame and tighten between the clamps. The saw frame should spring back and tighten the blade. The blade will make a pinging sound if it's at the correct tension.

Tip

Beeswax can be applied to the back of the blade to lubricate it and to aid cutting.

6 PREPARING TO CUT

Place the piece on the bench pin and hold it firmly with one hand. Position the saw frame at a 45-degree angle to the metal with the blade just outside the cutting line. Gently move the saw up and down until the blade cuts into the metal. Continue cutting while slowly moving the saw frame so it is at a 90-degree angle to the metal.

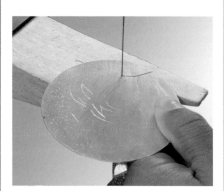

7 CUTTING

Relax the arm holding the saw frame and move it up and down. Don't push forwards with the saw frame because this will cause the blade to break. If you are having difficulties, check that the blade is tight and that it's inserted correctly. Cutting takes practice, and you will break lots of blades when learning, but it will get easier.

CUTTING OUT INTERIOR SHAPES

1 DRILLING

Cutting designs within a solid piece of metal is called 'piercing'. You can use this technique to cut independent shapes from one solid piece. Draw the designs on the metal and drill a 1mm (1/32in) hole (or larger) inside each shape.

2 PIERCING

Release one end of the blade from the saw frame and thread the piece through the hole and reattach the blade to the saw frame. Hold the saw frame at 90 degrees to the surface of the metal and begin cutting inside the line. Keep going until you have cut out the entire design.

FILING METAL

FILING IS THE LAST PROCESS BEFORE A PIECE IS FINISHED, AND IT IS IMPORTANT TO DEDICATE ENOUGH TIME TO IT. IT WOULD BE A SHAME TO SPEND A LONG TIME MAKING A PIECE OF JEWELLERY AND RUSH FINISHING IT. PIECES THAT HAVE BEEN SOLDERED, HAMMERED OR WORKED ON WILL NEED TO BE FILED BEFORE THEY CAN BE POLISHED. FILING CAN ALSO STRAIGHTEN UNEVEN EDGES AND SMOOTH CORNERS.

Investing in good jewellery files is essential and taking proper care of them will ensure that they last for a very long time. Store them in a dry place, preferably in a pouch, and don't use them on steel because this will dull the teeth. The most useful files are 15cm (6in) files and needle files; within these two categories there are a large selection of shapes and cut sizes. The cut size refers to the coarseness of the blades on the files and sizes start from 0-cut (coarse) up to 6-cut (fine). For larger pieces, start filing with a 15cm (6in) 0-cut file and work toward a 4-cut. Although there is a file for every job, a good starting point would be to buy a large half-round file and a set of twelve needle files and then add to your collection as necessary. When filing, apply pressure to the file with the piece resting on a surface.

TOOLS AND MATERIALS

FLAT FILE

HALF-ROUND FILE

RING CLAMP

SET OF TWELVE NEEDLE FILES

Tip
Use a ring clamp to help you grip small pieces for filing.

BASIC TECHNIQUES

USING A LARGE FILE
Use a large flat file to remove rough saw marks or deep scratches. Rest the piece on the bench pin and/or hold it in a ring clamp. If you are filing the edge, hold the file by the handle and keep it level with the surface of the metal. Push forwards, applying downward pressure and then release and pull back. The file only cuts in the forward motion. Continue in this way until you have removed all of the marks.

USING A NEEDLE FILE
Needle files are available in a range of sizes and shapes and are ideal for filing small areas. The file should match the shape you are filing, and the filing method is the same as using a larger file.

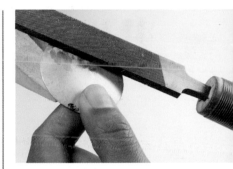

USING FLAT FILES
A large flat file can be used for filing the surface of a piece. Rest the piece on a bench pin and file in one direction while applying pressure. Keep the file flat on the surface until the area is filed.

ANNEALING, QUENCHING AND PICKLING

METAL IS MADE SOFTER BY HEATING IT WITH A TORCH, AND THIS PROCESS IS CALLED 'ANNEALING'. HARDENING OCCURS WHEN THE METAL IS HAMMERED. METAL CAN BE ANNEALED AND HAMMERED SEVERAL TIMES UNTIL THE DESIRED EFFECT IS ACHIEVED.

'Annealing' is when metal is heated to a particular temperature to make it more malleable for working. A torch is used to anneal, and there are a few types to choose from. A torch nozzle is sold separately from the gas tank, and some torches will only fit certain tanks. Oxygen is added to gas to make it burn; the temperature of the flame depends on the combination of oxygen and gas. Acetylene gas combined with oxygen is hotter than oxygen/propane or oxygen/natural gas, and any of these combinations is suitable for annealing metal. Be careful to avoid leakage when attaching the gas bottle to the torch and always turn off the gas at the bottle as well as the torch when you have finished working.

TOOLS AND MATERIALS

TORCH

30–CM (12–IN) SOLDERING BLOCK

15–CM (6–IN) SOLDERING BLOCK OR CHARCOAL BLOCK

GLASS JAR FOR WATER

BRASS OR COPPER TWEEZERS

OVENPROOF GLASS CONTAINER

PICKLE

REMOVING FIRESCALE

To prevent firescale on silver, apply flux each time the metal is annealed. Firescale can be removed from silver by heating with a low flame just enough to change the colour of the metal. Allow to air-cool, place in the pickle, and brush with a brass brush or steel wool. Repeat this process about eleven times and it will raise the fine silver to the surface and suppress the copper.

ANNEALING AND QUENCHING

1 PREPARING THE PIECE
Use two soldering blocks: a large one to protect the surface of the bench and a smaller one on which to rest the piece. Rest the piece on its edge against the side of the small soldering block to allow the heat to travel behind the piece.

2 ANNEALING
Turn the torch on and adjust it to a bushy flame. The hottest part of the flame is just beyond the blue tip. The flame should be big enough to cover most of the metal. Move the flame slowly across the surface until the trail of the flame leaves a rosy-pink colour – don't hold it in one position. The best way to know if the metal is annealed is to pay careful attention to the flame trail on the metal. This does take some experience, but if you're unsure, quench the metal, and if it bends easily, then it's annealed.

3 QUENCHING
Quenching is the process of cooling a hot piece of metal in water. Before quenching, leave the metal to cool for one minute. Use a glass jar to store water for quenching and take care when quenching, as the piece will be very hot. Use a pair of brass or copper tweezers to remove the piece from the soldering block and slowly place in the water. The piece will cool down immediately.

FIRESCALE

Alloyed metals that contain copper, such as silver and gold, can suffer from firescale when they are annealed. Firescale is a thin layer of copper that rises to the surface of the metal, and it is easily identifiable because of its reddish colour. It is particularly visible on silver if a white sheet is held against the surface. Through slow heating, it is possible to raise a fine layer of silver to the surface to cover the firescale; however, this layer can be removed by vigorous cleaning so it should only be done once the piece is finished. Firescale can also be filed away with a fine file or sandpaper.

Once annealed, the metal can be cooled by dipping it in water, known as 'quenching', or allowing it to air-cool. After soldering or annealing, allow the metal to cool for a few minutes before quenching. Quenching very hot metal will make a big splash and cause stress in the metal.

OXIDATION

Oxidation occurs when a piece of metal is heated with a flame or left exposed to the air. Oxidation caused by a flame is black in colour and can be removed with a solution called pickle. Pickle does not damage the metal. Each time a piece of metal is annealed it will become oxidized and can be safely placed in the pickle.

PICKLING

1 PREPARING THE PICKLE

Wear rubber gloves. Use a glass container with a secure lid or a slow cooker to keep the pickle warm. Follow the directions on the container for the mixing proportions. Always add acid to water and never add water to acid. In an ovenproof glass container, mix 1 part sulphuric acid to 10 parts water and, if using hot, allow the pickle to warm slightly. Pickle can also be used cold but will take a little longer to clean the metal. Use a separate pickle for gold and silver.

2 PLACING THE PIECE IN THE PICKLE

Remove the piece from the quenching water with a pair of brass or copper tweezers and place it in the pickle solution. Once the oxidation has been cleaned off – the metal will appear white – remove the piece and rinse thoroughly in water. Do not use steel tweezers to remove silver from the acid, as this will cause the silver to become copper-coated.

 HEALTH AND SAFETY WHEN PICKLING

'Pickling' is when oxidation is removed from the surface of metal by placing a piece in a bath of sulphuric acid mixed with water. Sulphuric acid is sold separately, and you will need to mix it with water yourself. It is very important to read and follow the health and safety procedures enclosed with the acid. When mixing acid wear rubber gloves and an apron. Use 1 part sulphuric acid to 10 parts water and always mix the two in a clean glass container with a secure lid. Always add acid to water – NEVER water to acid – and follow the mixing instructions on the package. This bath is commonly known as pickle, and it can be used hot or cold. Use a slow cooker or place it in a glass ovenproof bowl and put it in another pan so it is not directly heated. If acid spills on your skin, immediately run clean water over it. The skin may become red and irritated. Acid will leave a hole if spilled on clothing and will become visible in the next wash.

- **Wear rubber gloves and safety glasses**
- **Wear an apron**
- **Work in a ventilated area**
- **Label acid container and always store acid in a secure container**

SOLDERING

SOLDERING IS AN ESSENTIAL JEWELLERY-MAKING TECHNIQUE FOR JOINING PIECES OF METAL TOGETHER. COMPLICATED SHAPES WITH SEVERAL SIDES, SUCH AS BOXES, CAN BE CONSTRUCTED USING SOLDERING. SILVER SOLDER IS AN ALLOY OF ZINC AND STERLING SILVER AND, ONCE SOLDERED AND FINISHED, SEAMS WILL APPEAR INVISIBLE.

Soldering is the process of bonding metal using heat and solder. This can be either the same metal, for example, silver to silver, or different metals, such as gold to silver. Solder is a metal alloy of precious metal, copper and zinc. It is available in silver, or yellow or white gold, in a range of melting temperatures defined as 'hard', 'medium' and 'easy'. The metal is heated with a torch and, once the correct temperature is reached, the solder flows and fills the gaps between the joins. Solder forms a true bond with the metal, which makes the joint very strong, and afterwards it can be hammered and shaped as desired.

TOOLS AND MATERIALS

SOLDER

METAL SHEARS OR WIRE SNIPS

SOLDERING DISH

FLAT FILE

SMALL PAINTBRUSH

FLUX

CROSS-LOCKING TWEEZERS/
STRAIGHT TWEEZERS

TORCH

PROBE

SOLDERING BLOCK

WATER

PICKLE

FINE SANDPAPER

SOLDERING RULES

- Joints must fit perfectly without any visible gaps. It is worth spending time on getting the joints to fit.
- Joints must be clean, without any oxidation or dirt. Sandpaper can be used to sand the joint clean and key the surface to aid the application of the flux.
- Cut solder into small chips and put them in the flux dish. A small piece of solder will go a long way.
- Using excess solder will result in lots of cleaning up afterwards.
- The flame size should cover the piece, and heat should be evenly distributed.
- Hold the torch in one hand and a pair of tweezers in the other.

BASIC SOLDERING TECHNIQUE

1 CUTTING SOLDER

Solder can be bought in sheet, wire or strip form. Strips may need to be rolled thinner to make them easier to cut. Use a pair of metal shears or wire snips and cut several small pieces into the soldering dish.

2 MIXING FLUX

Prepare the flux by following the manufacturer's instructions; it should be a thick, creamy paste. If the flux is too runny, it will not work properly. Here, a cone of borax is being ground in borax dish. Tiny snips of solder are also placed in the borax so that they are coated with it.

If a piece has several joints, it is advisable to begin with a high-grade solder such as hard and use easy for the last joint. This is because each time a piece is heated there is a risk that existing joints will be reopened.

FLUX

Flux is applied to the joint to be soldered and works by protecting the metal from oxidation when heat is applied. Flux is available in powder or liquid forms. Powders will usually need to be mixed with water, while liquid can be used directly from the container. Each flux will differ slightly and you will find your own preference. When the metal is heated the water in the flux evaporates, leaving a glassy coating on the metal. At this stage the solder may have moved and will need to be pushed back into place, and the flux may become sticky. Two commonly used fluxes are: borax, which is available as a cone of powder that sits in a ceramic dish and is mixed with water to form a paste, and a borax-based compound that is already pre-mixed into a paste.

PREPARING TO SOLDER

You will need a large soldering mat to protect your work surface and a smaller block to sit on the mat. A soldering block may be charcoal, honeycomb or millboard, an asbestos substitute.

SOLDERED RING
by Vannetta Seecharran
This hollow silver ring was constructed with several pieces of sheet metal, soldered together.

TYPES OF SOLDER
• Hard solder melts at 773°C (1425°F) • Medium solder melts at 747°C (1390°F) • Easy solder melts at 771°C (1325°F)

IF THINGS GO WRONG
• If the solder flows away from the joint: The piece was not heated evenly and the solder flowed to the hottest part of the metal. Pickle to remove all oxidation, file away old solder and start again. • If the piece is green and black and the solder did not melt: A weak flame and prolonged heat have caused the flux to burn away. Pickle to remove all oxidation and start again.

3 PREPARING THE PIECE

File the ends of the pieces you want to join with a flat file until they sit flush together. To be sure, check if any light is coming through the joint by holding them up to a light source. Solder will not fill gaps; any gaps in the seam will be visible after soldering.

4 APPLYING FLUX

Use a small brush to apply flux to the seam on the inside and outside.

5 PLACING SOLDER

Coat the solder chips with flux. Use a pair of tweezers and place the solder in front of the seam. If the piece to be soldered is likely to move or roll, secure it with a pair of cross-locking tweezers.

6 HEATING

Hold the torch in one hand and a pair of tweezers or probe in the other hand. Use a flame large enough to heat the entire piece. Once heat is applied, the flux will begin to bubble, and the solder may move away from the seam. If this happens, continue to apply heat and move the solder back into place. If the flame is taken away from the piece, it will start to cool down immediately, and it may make soldering difficult. Move the flame across the entire piece until the colour begins to change and the solder melts. The solder will melt once the metal reaches the correct temperature. Remove the heat and leave the piece to cool for a few minutes.

7 CLEANING

Quench the piece in water (see page 26) and place in the pickle until all the oxidation has been removed. The metal will have a white finish; rinse it thoroughly in water to clean it and dry thoroughly. If the seam has not soldered, repeat the process.

SOLDERING FACE-TO-EDGE

1 KEYING THE SURFACE

When soldering onto a sheet of metal, use a fine sandpaper to key the surface. This will help the flux to hold onto the metal.

2 APPLYING FLUX

Apply flux to the surface of the sheet and on the edge that will sit on the surface.

3 SOLDERING

Place the solder chips around the outside of the shape so that they are sitting on the lip. Leave a 4mm (⅛in) gap between each solder chip and then heat. If there are any gaps on the joint after quenching and pickling, apply flux and new solder chips and solder once again. Repeat the process until there are no gaps. The lip can be cut off and then filed flush.

MARKING GRADES OF SOLDER

Mark the different grades of solder by bending one end to distinguish between the strips. So here, the complete square is hard solder.

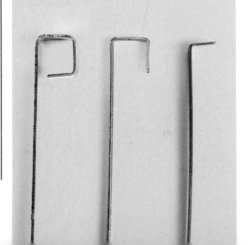

POLISHING METAL

POLISHING IS THE LAST AND MOST IMPORTANT STEP IN JEWELLERY MAKING, AND IT CAN BE DONE BEAUTIFULLY BY HAND OR WITH AN ELECTRIC MOTOR.

Polishing is the last stage of the finishing process and there are many different types of finish that can be achieved. One method is to use a polishing motor with a selection of polishing wheels. The first stage of polishing is to coat the wheel with a buffing compound, such as Tripoli. The second stage is to use a finishing compound, such as rouge.

The polishing motor is used for big pieces such as bracelets, pendants and some rings, but smaller pieces such as settings and earrings may need to be polished with a flexshaft motor. A flexshaft motor is a handheld electric machine with a foot pedal and is easier to use than a polishing motor.

Any motor will round off sharp edges, so if they are important to the piece, it's best to do the polishing by hand. Polishing by hand is an effective method of polishing, and some prefer it because you have more control and can maintain sharp edges.

TOOLS AND MATERIALS

WET AND DRY SANDPAPER

STEEL WOOL

BURNISHING TOOL OR TEASPOON

SAFETY GLASSES

DUST MASK

BUFFING WHEEL

BUFFING COMPOUND

FINISHING WHEEL

FINISHING COMPOUND

 HEALTH AND SAFETY

The first step before using the polishing motor is to tie back loose clothing, hair and anything else that could get caught in it.

POLISHING BY HAND

SANDING

If there are deep scratches or file marks, start with a course grade of sandpaper and use every grade towards a finer grade. Sand a flat surface by placing it flat on the sandpaper and sanding in a circular motion. Alternatively, hold a small piece in your hand and sand it with a small piece of sandpaper.

ACHIEVING TEXTURE

For a textured finish, stop sanding when you have reached the desired texture. For a satin finish, sand the piece with the finest sandpaper until it is scratch-free. Rub the piece vigorously with the steel wool until it has a slightly shiny, satin finish.

BURNISHING

'Burnishing' is when a metal tool is used to highlight an edge or other area of a piece. Use either a burnishing tool or the back of a teaspoon to rub an area several times until you achieve a high polish. This works well on edges, to contrast with a satin finish.

POLISHING MOTOR

1 ATTACHING THE MOP

Take care when using a polishing motor. Wear safety glasses and a dust mask and tie back loose hair or clothing. Screw the buffing wheel on in the opposite direction to the motor's rotation.

2 APPLYING THE COMPOUND

Turn on the machine and only use the lower quarter of the wheel. Hold the buffing compound on the buffing wheel for a few seconds until the wheel is well coated. Repeat the same procedure for the finishing compound.

3 BUFFING

Before polishing, your piece should be scratch-free and should have been sanded with the finest grade sandpaper. (Any scratches will be more visible after polishing.) Hold the piece firmly in both hands and never wrap anything around your finger. Stand in front of the wheel so you have a good view of the piece. Turn on the machine. Hold the piece on the wheel and move in an upward motion, against the rotation of the mop. Move the piece around so that it is all polished. Once finished, remove the buffing compound from the piece with soap and warm water; use a soft brush for the corners.

Tip
The machine spins very fast and can catch and throw back small pieces; therefore, pieces with sharp edges and difficult corners may be best polished by hand or with a flexshaft motor.

4 FINISHING

Repeat the previous step to apply the finishing compound. Keep rotating the piece to get an even finish – you may need to polish the same area two or three times for a mirrorlike finish. Note that sharp edges will become softer if you continue to polish. After polishing, wash the piece with soap and warm water to remove the compound.

FLEXSHAFT MOTOR

1 FLEXSHAFT ACCESSORIES

A flexshaft motor is an electric hand-held tool with a flexible cable connecting the hand-held device to the motor. There are many attachments available, ranging from sanding discs to polishing wheels.

POLISHING MOPS

From top to bottom:
(1) satin wheel for a satin finish; (2) sanding wheel for removing excess metal from surface; (3) polishing mops; (4) cone wheels for polishing the inside of rings.

2 METAL BURRS

Metal burrs can be attached to a flexshaft motor and are generally used for stone setting. There are many different shapes and sizes, and they can be used for cleaning and sanding.

3 POLISHING AND CLEANING

Attach the burr to the handpiece. Hold the handpiece against the metal and press the pedal with your foot. It takes some practice to control the speed; practice first on some scrap metal.

POLISHING METHODS

Wet and dry sandpaper can be used to polish metal once all the scratches have been removed with a file. It can be used wet or dry; the advantage of using it wet is that the metal dust can be washed away, and it also gives a smoother finish. The grit is usually marked on the back – the higher the number, the finer the grade. Start sanding with a coarse grade such as 240-grit and use every grade in between up to a fine grade, at which point you can switch to a polishing motor for a high shine or steel wool for a matt finish.

A barrel polisher has a barrel that vibrates and has metal or ceramic pieces inside called 'shots'. Jewellery pieces are placed in the barrel for a few hours, and the vibration causes the shots to rub against the metal, giving it a highly polished finish. This method of polishing is most popular with commercial jewellers for polishing cast pieces. A tumbler polisher works in the same way, but tumbles instead of vibrating.

Tip

Use a rubber wheel for final polishing.

LINKS: JUMP RINGS, EYE PINS AND HOOKS

LINKS ARE AN ESSENTIAL PART OF JEWELLERY MAKING AND CAN EASILY BE MADE WITH WIRE AND A FEW PAIRS OF JEWELLERY PLIERS. THEY CAN BE MADE TO ANY SIZE, SHAPE AND STYLE TO SUIT YOUR DESIGN.

A good selection of pliers is essential for making links, and the most useful types are round-nose, flat-nose, wire cutter and needle-nose. As you begin to work you may find that you will need additional pliers and you should get them as necessary. Always hold pliers by the handle, not too close to the nose. Making links takes lots of practice and may seem like an impossible task when you start out. Try to practise each technique until you perfect it, as this will add value to your pieces and make them look professional.

TOOLS AND MATERIALS

WIRE CUTTERS

ROUND-NOSE PLIERS

FLAT-NOSE PLIERS

JUMP-RING MANDREL OR 5MM (³⁄₁₆IN) WIDE ROD

1MM (18-GAUGE) HARD WIRE

0.8MM (20-GAUGE) HARD WIRE

FLAT NEEDLE FILE

STEEL BLOCK

PLANISHING HAMMER

EARRING HOOKS

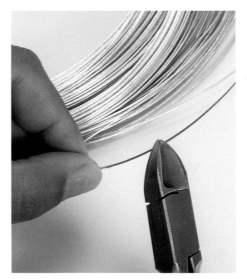

1 CUTTING THE WIRE
Earring hooks can be any size and style, and it is best to experiment with a few different lengths of wire before deciding on the final length. You will need 0.8mm (20-gauge) hard wire to make earring hooks, and for a standard size, a 5cm (2in) length. To make a pair, use wire cutters to cut two lengths.

2 FILING THE ENDS
File both ends of the wire flat with a needle file to remove the sharp tips.

WIRE

Wire is available in a variety of shapes and precious metals, however, the widest range is available in silver. Wires are sold either by the length or by gram weight, the most popular shapes being round, square, half round, oval and flat. Sizes range from around 0.5mm (24-gauge) to 3mm (8-gauge); however some suppliers may stock larger diameters. In the smaller sizes, wire is available in either 'hard' or 'soft' versions. Hard wire has been work-hardened and made stiff and is ideal for making earring hooks. Soft wire is very flexible and bends easily. Any of the styles are suitable for links, and what you choose depends on the design; however, flat, round and square profiles work especially well. The size of wire you use will depend on the size of the links. For links that are 1cm (½in) in diameter, 1.2mm (16-gauge) wire would be ideal.

Tips

• *Always point the pliers to the floor when you are cutting small pieces of wire, so that the offcut doesn't flick up into your eyes.*
• *Use a round pen or a small tube to make the loop on an earring hook.*

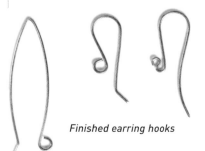

Finished earring hooks

3 USING THE ROUND PLIERS
Place the end of the wire in the pliers, about 6mm (¼in) from the tips. Use your thumb to push the wire around the nose while turning the pliers.

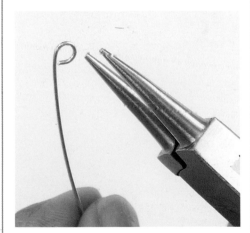

4 CREATING A LOOP
Turn the pliers until you have a complete circle. It should look like a backwards number nine.

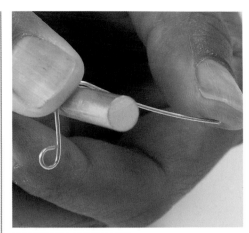

5 BENDING THE HOOK
Use a jump-ring mandrel or metal rod. Place the middle of the wire on top of the rod and use your other hand to push both ends of the wire together to make the hook.

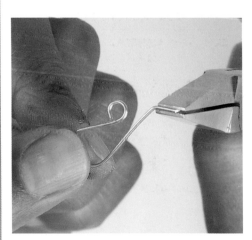

6 TURNING OUT THE END
Place the end of the wire in a pair of flat-nose pliers and turn the end outwards at a 45-degree angle. This will prevent the earring hook from falling out of the ear.

EYE-PIN LINK

1 CUTTING THE LENGTHS

Cut some 1-mm (18-gauge) hard wire to length. If you are making several links, cut all the wire at the same time. Once you have decided on the length of the finished link, add 8mm (⅜in) extra to accommodate the end hooks. Place the end of the wire in the round-nose pliers and bend around to make a complete circle so the wire looks like a number nine (see page 35). Keep the circle inside the nose of the pliers. If you are making several hooks, mark the spot on the nose that you will be using so each hook can be the same size.

2 TURNING BACK

Push the bottom of the nine against the other nose to make a question mark. It will take some practice to make it correctly, so do experiment on spare wire before using the final pieces.

MAKING AN S-HOOK

1 CUTTING AND SHAPING THE WIRE

S-hooks are suitable as clasps or links and can be made to any size from any wire size; the size of the pliers and length of the wire will determine the size of the hook. You may need to experiment with spare wire to get the correct size hook. Use 1mm (18-gauge) wire and cut a 16mm (⅝in) length. File both ends flat with a needle file. Use the very tip of the round-nose pliers to make a number nine shape on one end of the wire.

2 SHAPING THE WIRE

Next, place the wire in the pliers with the number nine shape facing up and resting against the nose of the pliers. Press the other end of the wire around the pliers to make a half S-shape.

3 BENDING AROUND THE PLIERS

Position the half S-shape of the wire in the round-nose pliers with the circle-ended number nine facing up. The number nine should be against the nose. Press the extra wire around the nose of the pliers.

4 ADDING THE FINISHING TOUCH

The end of the wire should be a few millimeters short of the bottom of the hook. Make a circle at the end of the wire (see page 35).

5 HAMMERING THE WIRE

The hook can be strengthened and flattened by gently hammering with a metal planishing hammer on a steel block. Place the hook on the steel block and hammer until the wire is a little flat and stiffer.

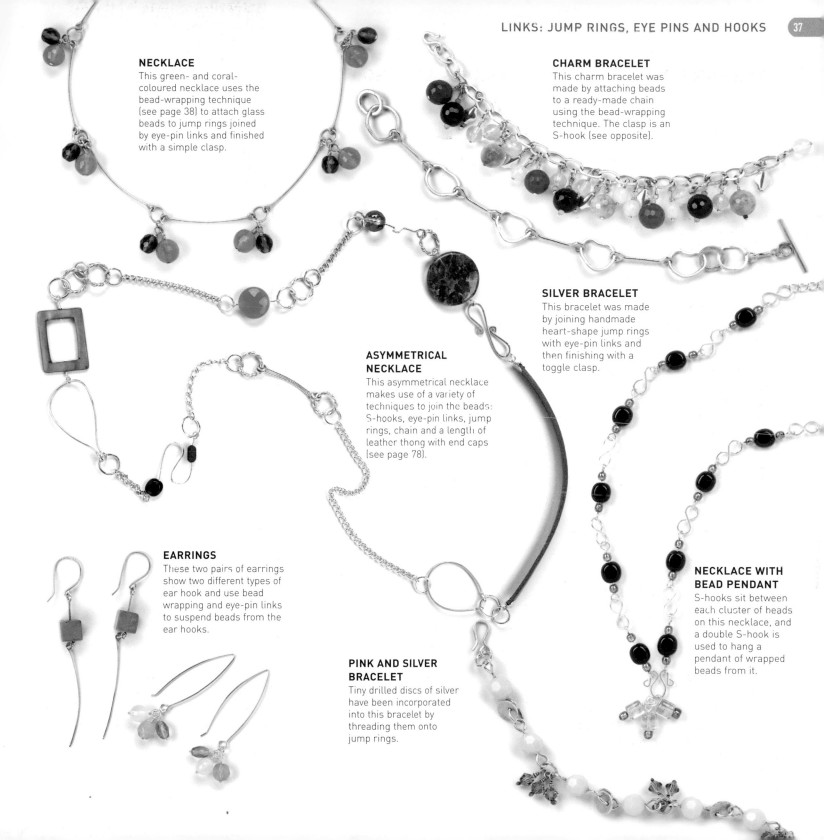

NECKLACE

This green- and coral-coloured necklace uses the bead-wrapping technique (see page 38) to attach glass beads to jump rings joined by eye-pin links and finished with a simple clasp.

CHARM BRACELET

This charm bracelet was made by attaching beads to a ready-made chain using the bead-wrapping technique. The clasp is an S-hook (see opposite).

SILVER BRACELET

This bracelet was made by joining handmade heart-shape jump rings with eye-pin links and then finishing with a toggle clasp.

ASYMMETRICAL NECKLACE

This asymmetrical necklace makes use of a variety of techniques to join the beads: S-hooks, eye-pin links, jump rings, chain and a length of leather thong with end caps (see page 78).

EARRINGS

These two pairs of earrings show two different types of ear hook and use bead wrapping and eye-pin links to suspend beads from the ear hooks.

PINK AND SILVER BRACELET

Tiny drilled discs of silver have been incorporated into this bracelet by threading them onto jump rings.

NECKLACE WITH BEAD PENDANT

S-hooks sit between each cluster of beads on this necklace, and a double S-hook is used to hang a pendant of wrapped beads from it.

BEAD WRAPPING

'BEAD WRAPPING' IS WHEN A LOOP IS MADE ON ONE END OF A BEAD SO THAT IT CAN BE ATTACHED TO A CHAIN TO MAKE A CHARM BRACELET OR MADE INTO A CLUSTER AND HUNG FROM AN EARRING HOOK.

Bead wrapping can be a satisfying process – however, it can be very difficult to get it to look neat. A head pin is used to wrap a bead – this is a pin that has a flat bottom on one end that keeps a bead from falling off. Head pins are available in precious and non-precious metals, from beading or jewellery suppliers. The head pin is placed through the hole of the bead and then wrapped to form a loop on the end. Once wrapped, the bead can be attached to a chain, used on an earring hook, or clustered together with other wrapped beads as a pendant. Head pins are available in different lengths and thicknesses, and you can put several beads on one pin.

THE BASIC TECHNIQUE

1 PREPARING THE BEAD
Thread the bead onto the head pin. If the bead has a big hole, use a seed bead as a stopper.

3 MAKING THE LOOP
Swap hands, holding the round-nose pliers in your weak hand and the needle-nose pliers in your strong hand. Use the tip of the needle-nose pliers and hold the end of the head pin. Wrap the wire over the nose of the pliers as shown.

5 TRIMMING THE EXCESS WIRE
Place the blade of the side cutters very close to the bead and trim the extra wire.

2 USING THE ROUND-NOSE PLIERS
Place the head pin in the round-nose pliers. Grip the pliers well so that the head pin does not fall off. Leaving a 4mm (³⁄₁₆in) gap between the top of the bead and the nose of the pliers, bend the wire around the nose of the pliers.

4 WRAPPING
Pull tightly on the end of the head pin and wrap the wire around itself several times, until you fill the space between the nose of the pliers and the bead. You should have a neat spiral. Don't wrap over what you have already done.

6 FINISHING
Use the needle-nose pliers to tuck in the extra wire. Straighten the loop with the round-nose pliers so that it's a perfect circle.

RIVETING

RIVETING IS OFTEN REFERRED TO AS A 'COLD' CONNECTION TECHNIQUE BECAUSE HEAT IS NOT REQUIRED. IT IS A USEFUL TECHNIQUE, ESPECIALLY WHEN YOU WANT TO COMBINE METAL WITH OTHER MATERIALS.

A rivet is a pin made from metal wire that is used to connect two materials together – the materials could be the same or different. For example, metal and leather could be connected by rivets, or metal and plastic, or two pieces of metal.

There are three main types of rivets: standard rivets, invisible rivets and tube rivets. A standard rivet has a 'mushroomed' head and sits proud of the surface; an invisible rivet blends with the surface; and a tube rivet is made from tubing with both ends flared.

Rivets can be used to secure two pieces together or to allow movement between two pieces. Rivets are used when it is not possible to solder pieces together or when one of the materials being joined is not metal. The material being riveted must be 'sandwiched' between two pieces of metal so that the rivet head sits on a secure surface and cannot pull through.

The essential rule for making a good rivet is that the drill bit and the rivet wire or tube must be exactly the same size so that the rivet fits snugly in the hole. If the rivet wire moves freely, the rivet will not hold properly. The head of the wire is flared at both ends with a riveting hammer, just enough to keep the rivet from falling out.

TOOLS AND MATERIALS

DRILL BIT

METAL WIRE

CALIPERS/MEASURING TOOL

CLOTH

FLAT NEEDLE FILE

RIVETING HAMMER

CENTRE PUNCH

FLAT-NOSE PLIERS

CUTTERS

FLEXSHAFT MOTOR AND SMALL CONE OR BURR HEADS

METAL TUBING

TUBING CUTTER

SCRIBER

ROUND PUNCH

SANDPAPER

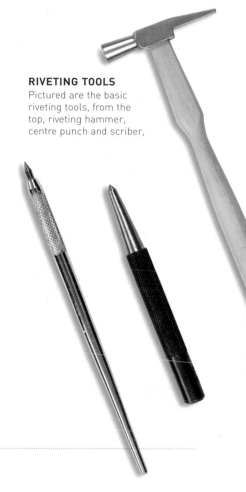

RIVETING TOOLS
Pictured are the basic riveting tools, from the top, riveting hammer, centre punch and scriber.

STANDARD RIVET

1 PIECES TO BE RIVETED
For this example, a patterned piece of wood will be riveted into a silver casing.

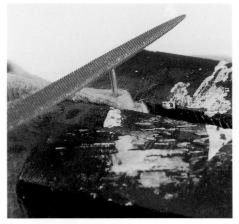

2 PREPARING THE WIRE

Check that the drill bit and wire are exactly the same diameter. Cut a length of wire twice the length of the total thickness of the pieces you are riveting. Wrap the wire in a cloth and secure in a vice with just the tip of the wire visible. File the end flat with a needle file.

3 FLARING THE END

Use a riveting hammer to flare the end of the wire by hitting it at an angle evenly all around. The face of the hammer should be hitting the edge of the wire. Rub your fingers over the head of the wire to ensure it is flaring correctly – it should feel mushroom-shape. Once it is flared, leave it in the vice until you are ready to use it.

4 MARKING THE HOLE

Place the metal you want to rivet on a steel surface and tap the centre punch where you want the rivet, just enough to make a little dent. The dent will guide the drill bit into the correct place.

5 DRILLING THE TOP PIECE

Place the metal on a wooden block and drill a hole in the metal. It's important that the drill bit is exactly the same diameter as the rivet.

6 DRILLING ALL THE PIECES

Next, place the drilled piece in position and secure all of the pieces to be riveted with clear tape. In this case, the wooden piece is sandwiched between two pieces of metal. Drill all the pieces together.

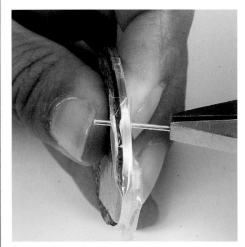

7 INSERTING WIRE

Remove the wire from the vice and thread it through the holes, with the flared head resting on the top piece of metal. Use a pair of flat-nose pliers to pull the wire through both pieces.

8 CUTTING THE WIRE

Snip the excess wire protruding from the bottom of the piece with a pair of cutters, leaving 1mm (1/32in) of wire above the surface.

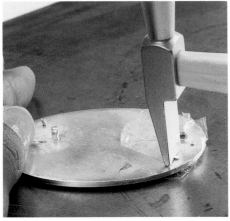

10 FINISHING

Use the narrow end of the riveting hammer and gently hammer the wire until it is flared. Now hammer the riveted head with the face of the hammer. Sand the rivet for an even finish and remove the tape.

Tip

To avoid hammer marks on the metal, protect the surface with clear tape.

FINISHED BROOCH

This brooch was made by riveting laser-patterned plywood with silver sheet.

9 FILING

File just the tip of the wire to remove the sharp tip but leaving some wire protruding from the surface.

RIVETED BROOCH

by Vannetta Seecharran

This brooch was made with two sheets of pierced silver, which were riveted together, allowing the steel balls inside to move freely along the slots.

RIVETED CLASP
by Vannetta Seecharran
The silver clasp on this bracelet was riveted to the woven material using a standard rivet.

FLUSH RIVET

1 PIECES TO BE RIVETED
Some Perspex sheet is to be riveted between two pieces of silver.

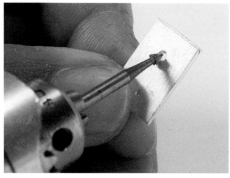

2 BEVELLING THE HOLE
A flush rivet is made in the same way as a standard rivet, except that the hole is bevelled so the mushroomed head sits just below the surface of the metal.

Repeat Steps 2 to 6 as for the standard rivet. Use a very small cone or round shaped burr with the flexshaft motor (see page 33) and bevel the drill hole on one side of your piece, or, if you would like a flush head on both sides, bevel the top and bottom holes.

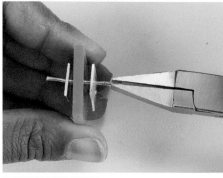

3 INSERTING WIRE
Insert the wire through all the pieces with the flared head resting on the top piece of metal.

4 FILING FLUSH
Repeat Steps 8 to 10 as for a standard rivet. The rivet head can be finished with fine sandpaper.

RIVETING WITH TUBING

1 CUTTING THE TUBING

As for the other rivets, all the pieces to be connected must be drilled, and the tubing must have a tight fit through the hole. Cut the tube 2mm (1/16in) longer than the width of the pieces being riveted. The tube can be placed inside a tubing cutter or may rest on the bench pin.

2 FLARING THE TUBING

Insert the tube into the hole with an equal distance of the tubing on either side. Use a scriber to press against the edges of the tubing and flare the edges. Repeat for the other end of the tube. Flaring in this way may be enough to secure the tube.

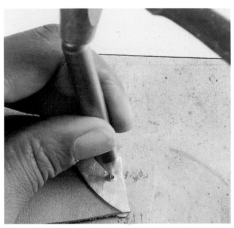

3 USING A FLARING PUNCH

Placing the tube over a rounded form and hammering the other side with a round punch can flare the edge further. This can also be done on a steel block with a small round punch.

MOVABLE RIVET

1 PIECES TO BE RIVETED

These shaped pieces of silver will be attached with a movable rivet to make an earring.

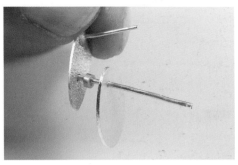

2 PREPARATION

As for the standard rivet, the wire must fit snugly in the hole, and the short tube that will separate the elements should fit around the wire. Cut a 1mm (1/32in) length of tubing and sand both ends flat. (Flat ends are important so that the pieces hang straight.) Mushroom the head of the rivet and thread the pieces together so that the tubing is sandwiched between the two pieces of metal.

3 FINISHING

Cut the extra wire and flare the end. Be careful not to over-hammer, as this may cause the rivet to become tight and prevent movement. Follow Steps 9 to 10 for a standard rivet to finish.

MOVABLE RIVET

The two pieces of riveted metal can move freely on the finished earring.

SHAPING METAL

METAL CAN BE SHAPED INTO CURVES, ANGLES AND OTHER INTERESTING SHAPES BY HAMMERING IT OVER A FORMING TOOL. THE VARIETY OF FORMING TOOLS AND HAMMERS AVAILABLE IS EXTENSIVE, RANGING FROM CURVED SHAPES FOR MAKING DOMES TO MANDRELS FOR CREATING RINGS.

Shaping metal is an essential technique in jewellery making. Metal can be manipulated into almost any shape or design by hammering it over a forming tool. For example, rings are made from a strip of metal hammered over a ring mandrel and a dome shape can be achieved by hammering over a mushroom stake.

The range of forming tools is extensive; however, some of the more common ones include mallets, metal stakes, steel blocks, sandbags and doming punches. A rawhide, wooden or nylon mallet can be used to hammer a piece of metal over any forming tool to create curves, angles and domes. The mallets used for forming are softer than the metal so they don't mark the surface. Once annealed, metal can be hammered and shaped as many times as necessary to achieve the desired shape.

TOOLS AND MATERIALS

STRIPS OF METAL

VICE

RING MANDREL

RAWHIDE MALLET

FLAT-NOSE PLIERS

MUSHROOM STAKE

DOMING BLOCK AND PUNCHES

FLAT-HEAD METAL HAMMER

RING
by Vannetta Seecharran
The pieces used to create this ring were fabricated from sheets of silver, and the curved sides were shaped on a mandrel.

FORMING TECHNIQUES

1 HAMMERING A STRIP
Anneal the metal before starting to form it (see page 26). Secure the ring mandrel in a vice. Use a rawhide mallet and hold the end of the handle. Place one end of the strip on the mandrel and apply a few hammer strokes in a downward motion until the end begins to curve.

2 MAKING A CIRCLE
To make a complete circle, hammer the other side of the strip as described in Step 1. The metal should make contact with the mandrel at all times. Once the strip is a 'C' shape, bring the ends together with a pair of flat-nose pliers. The ends should meet, and this seam can be soldered (see page 28).

WORK-HARDENING METAL

'Work-hardening' is a process of strengthening metal by putting it under stress, and this can be done by hammering, stretching or extruding it. The more metal is hammered, the harder it will become; however, it can then be annealed to reduce the stress and then further hammered. If metal becomes too stressed through working, it will begin to split; therefore, it is important to anneal it frequently.

MALLETS

A rawhide mallet is used to shape a piece of metal over a mandrel. A nylon mallet can be used to either shape or sink metal into a form.

STAKES

Stakes are metal shapes that are used for forming. There is a range of shapes available, including ring mandrels, mushroom stakes and spoon stakes. When metal is hammered over a stake it will take on the shape of the stake. Choosing the correct stake will depend on the shape you are aiming for. For example, you can make a dome by hammering over a mushroom stake; a ring mandrel is used for making circles.

3 MAKING A ROUNDED SHAPE

Once the ring is soldered, place it back on the mandrel. Begin hammering from the seam and aim the strokes onto the side of the mandrel, in a brushing downward motion. Move the ring around the mandrel and continue hammering until it is round.

Tip
Wrap the handle of the mandrel with a cloth before securing in a vice to prevent it from being damaged.

MAKING A DOMED SHAPE

Any shape can be hammered over a mushroom stake to give it a slight domed effect. Place the metal on the stake and use a rawhide mallet to 'stroke' the metal in a downwards brushing motion until you reach the desired shape.

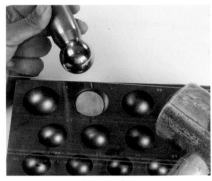

USING A DOMING BLOCK

Small shapes can be domed in a doming block. Place the shape in the largest indentation. Using a flat-head metal hammer, hammer the head of the doming punch until the metal touches the bottom of the dome. (When you hear a metallic sound you will know that it is touching the bottom of the dome.) Always start with a large indentation and work down the sizes until you reach the required size. After shaping in a few domes, the metal may become work-hardened and will require annealing before continuing. A rawhide mallet can also be used to hammer the doming punch.

CHAPTER 2

PLASTIC
AND RUBBER

This chapter explores the ways in which plastic and rubber can be used in jewellery making. Rubber can be folded and intricately cut for a suprising range of shapes and applications, while plastic can be transformed by dyeing, laminating and printing, and shaped with the application of heat.

NECKLACE *(opposite)*
by Rosie Wolfenden
Dinosaur necklace made from acrylic and metal alloy.

BANGLES *(top right)*
by Lesley Strickland
Hand thermo-formed cellulose acetate bangles.

RING *(centre left)*
by Patrizia Iacino
Recycled rubber bands in a sterling silver base.

COLLECTION *(centre right)*
by Andre Ribeiro
Black rubber and diamond jewellery.

PLASTIC AND RUBBER PROPERTIES

'PLASTIC' IS A TERM USED TO DESCRIBE A RANGE OF SYNTHETIC AND SEMI-SYNTHETIC PRODUCTS OF POLYMERIZATION. THE PROCESS OF POLYMERIZATION OCCURS WHEN MOLECULES ARE COMBINED, THROUGH HEAT OR PRESSURE, TO FORM LONG CHAINS THAT LINK TOGETHER AND RESULT IN A SOLID MATERIAL. THE RAW MATERIAL IS MADE FROM PETROLEUM, AND OTHER COMPOUNDS ARE ADDED TO ACHIEVE THE DESIRED RESISTANCE, ELASTICITY AND COLOUR.

Sheet plastic lends itself well to making jewellery. It is widely available from plastic suppliers, and scrap pieces can be collected from sign makers or plastic manufacturers. Because of its low cost, it can be used to make prototypes or finished pieces of jewellery. The wide range of transparent and opaque colours is excellent for making bold, expressive jewellery. Multiple shapes are usually cut on a laser machine; however, tools used for working with metal can be used for cutting, filing and finishing.

Plastic has associated health risks and releases toxic fumes when burning

RUBBER STRIPS AND RODS

PERSPEX SHEETS

LATEX SHEETS

and reheating; therefore, it is necessary to wear the appropriate protective clothing when working with it. Heating techniques such as vacuum forming and heat forming should be done in a ventilated area, and you should wear a mask that protects against fumes.

Rubber can be either natural or synthetic. Natural rubber is collected from rubber trees, and the raw material is usually made into latex. Synthetic rubber, often referred to as 'industrial' rubber, is derived from petroleum. Most rubber is synthetic.

Rubber is used to make a wide variety of products ranging from household items to industrial products. It is a somewhat unlikely material for jewellery making, and many jewellers shy away from it because of its industrial associations. However, it's an inexpensive and easily accessible material, which makes it good for experimentation.

OVERHEATING
A characteristic drawback when working with some plastics is that they are easy to damage by overheating, causing loss of colour, a bubbled texture and a grainy finish. To prevent this, you need to constantly monitor the temperature.

DESIGNING WITH PLASTIC AND RUBBER

Qualities Plastic is colourful, transparent or opaque, strong yet flexible. Rubber is soft, smooth and stretchy.

Application The affordability of plastic and rubber lends itself well to experimentation and trying new ideas. The lightness allows for making big and bold jewellery pieces without them becoming too heavy. The translucent qualities of some plastics can be advantageous because coloured sheets can be laminated together and carved into three-dimensional shapes to create optical interest.

Rubber can be cut and folded into a variety of patterns to make bracelets, earrings and necklaces. Pearls and beads can be encased around sheets and contrast well with the texture of rubber and latex.

Combining with other materials Plastic can be combined with most materials, including metal, wood, fabric and rubber. It is especially effective when combined with metal and wood.

Where to look for inspiration Take a look at the websites below for inspiration from jewellers working with plastics and rubber.
- **Arthur Hash, United States**
www.arthurhash.com
Working with a variety of materials, often plastics. There is a great blog on his website.
- **Ela Bauer, Netherlands**
www.elabauer.com
Silicone rubber and mixed-media works.
- **Rachel McKnight, Ireland**
www.rachelmcknight.com
Polypropylene and acrylic jewellery with cold connections.

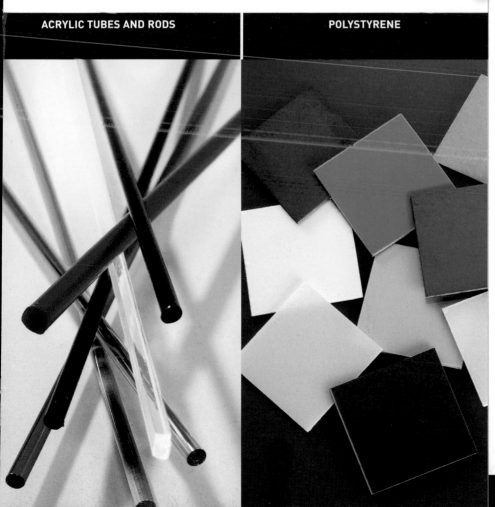

ACRYLIC TUBES AND RODS

POLYSTYRENE

CUTTING AND PIERCING PLASTIC

PLASTICS ARE USUALLY SOLD IN LARGE SHEETS, IN A RANGE OF COLOURS AND THICKNESSES AND CAN BE CUT TO SIZE BY SCORING AND BREAKING. THEY CAN BE USED TO CONSTRUCT THREE-DIMENSIONAL SHAPES AND JOINED TOGETHER WITH A LIQUID SOLVENT.

There are several ways to cut plastic, including using a band saw, scoring and breaking, and cutting with a jewellery saw. You could also use a laser cutter to cut multiples of the same shape. Each type of plastic will respond differently to the cutting methods. For example, polystyrene is flexible, and its dust is sticky and may clog the blade of the cutting tools, whereas acrylic is brittle and the dust is looser. Plastic sheets are best suited to designs that have big, bold shapes because intricate shapes may break off. A jewellery saw is perfect for cutting shapes from plastic – use a 1/0 blade for cutting 2mm (¹⁄₁₆in) sheet and a 1 or 2 blade for cutting 3mm (¹⁄₈in) or thicker sheets.

GIRL ON A SWING
by Rosie Wolfenden
This pendant was laser-cut from acrylic sheet, a good way to create multiples of a particular design.

TOOLS AND MATERIALS

SHEET PLASTIC

KNIFE

RULER

METAL BLOCK

SCRIBER

SAW BLADES

SAW FRAME

DRILL BITS

Tip
Transfer designs onto plastic by either drawing directly on the plastic or gluing on a paper template. If you use a paper template, glue the edges carefully because the saw blade will lift any loose paper, and it will become difficult to follow your design. If the blade gets stuck in the plastic, use a lighter to heat the section of the blade just above the plastic – the heat will release the blade.

SCORE AND BREAK

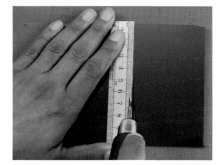

1 SCORING
Position the ruler where you would like to cut the plastic. Using a sharp knife, score against the edge of the ruler several times until you have scored a quarter of the depth of the plastic.

2 POSITIONING
After scoring, place the plastic on the edge of a table with the score line overhanging the edge slightly. Place a heavy metal block or a metal ruler on the edge of the score line.

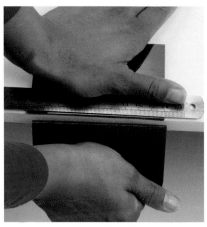

3 SNAPPING
Place one hand on the block or ruler and hold the edge of the plastic in the other. Press firmly and snap the plastic. It should snap along the scored line. If the plastic doesn't snap, score it a few more times and use a heavier weight on top such as a steel block.

BASIC SAWING

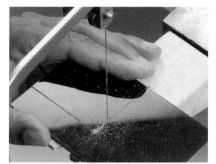

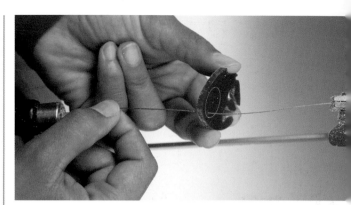

1 SCORING

Score a line on the plastic with a scriber using a straight edge such as a ruler – include a right angle.

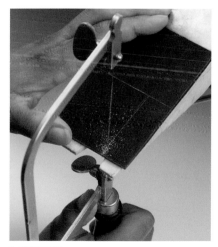

2 CUTTING

Hold the plastic on the bench pin. Position the blade outside the score line at right angles to the plastic and move the saw with a gentle up and down motion while pushing forwards. Don't move the saw too quickly or the friction will heat up the blade and melt the plastic, causing the blade to get stuck. (See Cutting and piercing metal, page 22.)

3 CUTTING A RIGHT ANGLE

Once you have reached the corner continue to move the blade up and down several times in the same place until it can move freely. Turn the plastic on the bench pin so the blade is facing the direction of the line and continue cutting.

PIERCING OUT INTERIOR SHAPES

1 DRILLING

Drill a hole at least 1mm (1/32in) in diameter inside your design. The hole needs to be large enough for you to thread the saw blade through it. You can use an electric or a manual drill.

2 PREPARING TO CUT

Release one end of the blade from the saw frame and thread the blade through the hole with the design facing up. Once threaded, secure the blade in the saw frame once again.

3 PIERCING

Place the piece on the bench pin, with the blade inside the 'V' shape on the pin and saw close to, but not on, the line. Keep the line in view as it will serve as a guide for cutting.

FILING PLASTIC

FILES ARE DEFINED BY THEIR CUT, SHAPE AND SIZE. CHOOSING THE CORRECT FILE CAN MAKE THE JOB EASIER. TO START WITH, YOU WILL NEED A 15CM (6IN) HALF-ROUND FILE AND A SET OF TWELVE NEEDLE FILES; BUILD UP YOUR COLLECTION FROM THERE.

Finishing a piece of jewellery is the most important part of the making process and requires time and patience. It's crucial to pay attention to the area that you are filing and to always keep an eye on the edges. Plastic is very soft, and it doesn't take much to round off a sharp corner. Jewellery files are great to use on plastic, but they will quickly clog up and will need to be cleaned often with a wire brush. You can sand very rough edges on a belt sander, but it will only take a few seconds to remove a large amount of material – for a small amount, use a regular file. Sheet plastics and resin shapes can be filed using the same method and tools; however, resin is a denser material, and it will take longer to file. The dust produced from plastic is toxic, so always wear a dust mask when filing.

TOOLS AND MATERIALS

RING CLAMP

15CM (6IN) FLAT FILE

15CM (6IN) HALF-ROUND FILE

SET OF NEEDLE FILES

Tip
Clean the file
If the file becomes clogged up with dust clean it with a wire brush.

BRACELET
by Rachel McKnight
This bracelet was pierced from plastic sheet and then carefully filed. Needle files would have to be used for the very fine fretwork.

BASIC TECHNIQUES

USING A LARGE FLAT FILE
Hold the piece firmly against the bench pin with your hand or, for a smaller piece, grip in a ring clamp. Hold the file level against the edge of the piece and push forwards with some force. Continue this motion until you have removed all the scratches. Move the file along the whole length of the edge to smooth the rough marks; never file in just one place.

USING A HALF-ROUND FILE
The flat side of the file is good to use on large concave surfaces, while the round side is ideal for smaller, rounded surfaces, such as an interior shape. Hold the piece you are filing on the bench pin. For a cut-out interior shape (such as a circle), place the half-round side of the file inside and push forwards in an upward movement. Keep the file level and moving along the surface. Never file in only one position, as this will create notches in the surface.

USING A NEEDLE FILE
Hold the piece on the bench pin, place the file inside the shape, and file until you have removed all the marks from piercing. Generally, the needle file shape should match the shape that you are filing. For example, round files are used for rounded shapes, square files are used for corners and flat files are used for flat surfaces.

POLISHING PLASTIC

POLISHING PLASTIC IS AN EXCELLENT WAY TO GIVE A PROFESSIONAL FINISH TO YOUR PIECES, AND IT CAN EASILY BE DONE BY HAND OR WITH AN ELECTRIC MOTOR.

Most plastics can be polished to a shiny or matt surface. Plastic is a soft material, and so pieces will become scratched over time, but it can be repolished many times. Each type of plastic will look slightly different once polished. Plastics such as acrylic can be polished to a mirrorlike surface, whereas it's more difficult to polish styrene to this extent. Resins need to be completely cured before polishing on a motor because the compound will become embedded if the surface is tacky. Special compounds and mops are used to polish plastics – they are grittier than the compounds used on metal. Before a piece can be polished it must be sanded with wet and dry sandpaper, starting with a coarse grade such as 320-grit and using every grade up to 800-grit before moving onto polishing.

TOOLS AND MATERIALS

DIFFERENT GRADES OF SANDPAPER

SAFETY GLASSES

DUST MASK

POLISHING MOTOR

BUFFING WHEEL

BUFFING COMPOUND

FINISHING WHEEL

FINISHING COMPOUND

ACRYLIC BANGLES
by Rachel McKnight
These bangles were highly polished to create a shiny surface.

SANDING

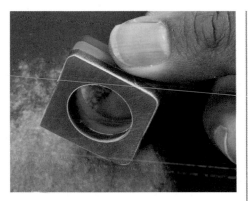

USING SANDPAPER
Flat surfaces can be sanded face down on sandpaper. Place the piece on the paper and sand in a circular motion until all the scratches are gone. If there are deep scratches, start sanding with a coarse grit and work towards a fine grit. For edges and hard-to-reach areas, tear off a piece of paper, fold it to a comfortable size and sand in a circular motion.

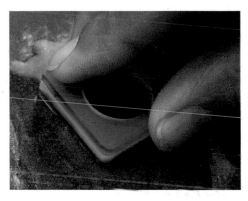

ACHIEVING A SATIN FINISH
Add a little water to the sandpaper and sand in a circular motion until the piece is smooth.

Tip
For a smooth matt surface: Once you have sanded with the finest sandpaper, wrap a nylon stocking around your hand and rub the piece vigorously. (You can use any other fabric that has a slight texture.)

BUFFING AND POLISHING

1 APPLYING BUFFING COMPOUND
Put on your safety glasses and dust mask. Attach the buffing wheel to the motor. Turn on the motor, hold the buffing compound with both hands and apply it to the buffing wheel. Coat the wheel well with the compound. Jewellery stores may not stock plastic polishing compound; however, stores selling sculpture materials usually stock them. (See page 32 for advice on using a polishing motor.)

2 BUFFING
Hold the piece firmly with both hands and press against the buffing wheel. Keep the piece moving and try not to hold it in one place as this can give you an uneven finish and remove too much material from one area. Once you have finished buffing, use soap and warm water to remove the compound from the piece.

⚠ HEALTH AND SAFETY

Safety is most important, and so the first step before using the polishing motor is to tie back loose clothing, hair and anything else that could get caught in it.

3 FINISHING POLISH
Attach the finishing wheel to the motor. Turn on the motor and coat the wheel with the finishing compound. Hold the piece firmly and polish the entire surface of your piece. Again, use soap and warm water to remove the compound from the piece.

THE FINISHED PIECE
This acrylic ring was first sanded and then polished to a shiny mirrorlike surface.

OVERLAY AND INLAY

SHEETS OF THE SAME PLASTIC CAN BE JOINED TOGETHER WITH A LIQUID SOLVENT TO INCREASE THE THICKNESS OR TO CREATE DECORATIVE EFFECTS. THE SOLVENT CREATES A CHEMICAL BOND BETWEEN THE SHEETS THAT WILL WITHSTAND CARVING AND FILING.

Plastic sheets can be joined together by their edges to create three-dimensional structures. Plastic is joined with a liquid solvent, a chemical that melts the plastic surfaces together and forms a true bond between the sheets. Pieces of plastic can also be inlaid via a carved hole or overlaid and bonded with solvent. Inlay pieces must fit perfectly, without any gaps; the solvent will not fill the gaps. Once bonded, the plastic can be cut and filed for a smooth finish. Over time the seam between the sheets will recede and become visible. It is necessary to bear this in mind when constructing with plastic – you may want to minimize the amount of joins in a piece. The solvent is a clear liquid and can be applied with a small brush. It will evaporate over time so store it with the lid tightly closed. Keep the container away from children and pets.

TOOLS AND MATERIALS

PAINTBRUSH

LIQUID SOLVENT

SANDPAPER

SHEETS OF PLASTIC

PLASTIC RODS

DRILL BIT

FILE

Tip
When constructing a three-dimensional form, be diligent in filing the edges straight so they sit flush, without gaps. The solvent will not fill gaps, and correcting a mistake is difficult and time-consuming.

OVERLAYING

Pieces can be 'welded' together to increase thickness or for decorative effects. Position the pieces in place and apply the solvent all around the edge of the top shape.

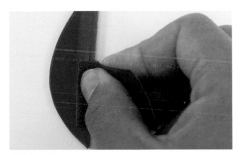

1 KEYING
Use a fine grade sandpaper to lightly sand the surfaces that you want to join. This process is called 'keying', and it will help to increase the bond between the two pieces of plastic.

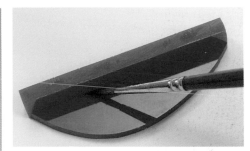

2 JOINING TWO SHEETS TOGETHER
Place the two pieces together and adjust their positions. Dip a clean brush in the liquid solvent and apply along the edge of the piece. The liquid will seep into the joint and take a few minutes to dry. Once it is dry, it will create a permanent bond between the two pieces and can be filed flush. The pieces being joined need to fit well without any gaps.

THE FINISHED PIECE
To create this brooch, pieces of acrylic sheet were welded together to create a hollow three-dimensional shape.

INLAY

1 CUTTING SHAPES FOR INLAY
Small pieces of plastic can be inlaid into a larger piece. In this example, plastic rods are inlaid into a shaped piece of plastic sheet, but any shape can be inlaid into another as long as it is a perfect fit. Cut a piece of rod that is longer than the depth of the piece of plastic you are inserting it into. Next, drill a hole in the piece of plastic the same diameter as the rod. The rod should fit tightly into the hole without any gaps. The solvent will not work if there are gaps between the pieces.

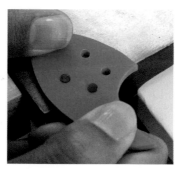

2 INSERTING INLAY PIECES
Insert a piece of rod into one of the holes you have drilled and press firmly so that it sits flush with the underside of the plastic. Repeat the process for all the other pieces you wish to inlay.

3 APPLYING SOLVENT
Once all your pieces of inlay are in place, use a small brush to apply solvent around the edge of the rods. Once it is dry, you can file the rods to the same level as the plastic.

4 ATTACHING TWO PIECES
Before attaching two pieces together, you must ensure that the edges meet exactly, without any gaps. It is worth spending some time on this before applying the solvent. Place the pieces next to each other and apply the solvent along the join. Leave to dry for a few minutes. Once it is dry, the piece can be filed and sanded.

FINISHED PENDANT
This opaque orange pendant has been inlaid with transparent acrylic rod and joined side by side with a piece of transparent sheet.

FINISHED BANGLE
To make this bangle, a strip of acrylic has been heat formed, and three holes drilled and bevelled into it. The beads are welded into the bevelled holes.

ADDING BEADS

1 DRILLING THE HOLE
Plastic beads can be attached to the surface of a piece of plastic jewellery. Drill a hole with a round drill bit on the exact spot where you would like to attach the bead. Next, bevel the hole using a triangular burr on a flexshaft motor (see page 33) until the bead sits a quarter of its depth in the hole.

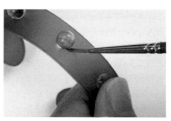

2 SECURING THE BEADS
Now place the bead in the hole and apply the solvent all around the edge. Once the solvent is dry, the beads will be firmly attached.

LAMINATING ACRYLIC

YOU CAN INCREASE THE THICKNESS OF ACRYLIC SHEETS BY STACKING AND LAMINATING THEM. ONCE LAMINATED, THE SHEETS WILL APPEAR AS ONE BLOCK THAT CAN BE CARVED, SHAPED AND POLISHED.

Acrylic sheets can be stacked and laminated together using a solvent such as Tensol 70 or Acrifix. Always refer to the manufacturer's instructions for making up the solvent and follow any safety advice carefully. Wear a dust mask and rubber gloves and work in a well-ventilated area. Protect your work surface with newspaper.

Some solvents will shrink by 10 per cent once they are cured (dry), so add an extra 10 per cent of material to your design. Once cured, the edges can be cut to the correct size.

By laminating sheets together a block of plastic can be created to carve, from which any type of jewellery can be made. A very thick block may be difficult to cut by hand and may need to be cut with a bandsaw. For the same reason, the initial shaping may need to be done with a belt sander; a file and sandpaper can be used for finishing off.

TOOLS AND MATERIALS

- DUST MASK
- RUBBER GLOVES
- PLASTIC CONTAINER
- MIXING STICKS
- LAMINATING SOLVENT
- ACRYLIC SHEETS
- STEEL BLOCK

BASIC TECHNIQUE

1 POURING LIQUID OVER THE SHEETS

Clean the sheets of acrylic with mineral spirits to remove any dust and grease. Mix the solvent according to the manufacturer's instructions and follow the user guide for its application. Many solvents are self-levelling and are best applied by pouring them over one face of the sheet to overhang the edges.

2 STACKING SHEETS

Stack another sheet of acrylic on top of the mixture and repeat the same process until you have stacked all the sheets you wish to laminate.

Tip
To avoid air bubbles between layers, slide the sheets together from the side.

3 APPLYING PRESSURE

Place a steel block over the stacked sheets and leave them to cure. Two hours after application the sheets can be handled carefully; however, complete curing only occurs after twenty-four hours by which time the sheets should appear seamless and totally transparent.

LAMINATED EARRINGS
by Vannetta Seecharran
Laminated together and cut to size, a transparent sheet has been sandwiched between two opaque sheets to make these earrings.

THE FINISHED PIECE
The finished sheets should have bonded together completely and should be completely transparent, without bubbles.

HEAT FORMING

ACRYLIC SHEETS AND RODS CAN BE FORMED AND SHAPED BY HEATING THEM IN A CONVENTIONAL OVEN. IN THIS WAY, YOU CAN ACHIEVE A RANGE OF INTERESTING SHAPES. THE ACRYLIC CAN BE REHEATED AND FORMED MANY TIMES UNTIL YOU GET THE DESIRED EFFECT.

Thermoplastics such as high-impact polystyrene, polypropylene and acrylic can be heat-formed successfully. Acrylic is the best plastic to use for small objects because it is easy to work with and produces the best finish.

Most plastics can be heat-formed in a conventional oven. The correct amount of heat alters the structure of the plastic, making it malleable and easy to mould. Generally the plastic will harden within minutes; however, the hardening time will depend on the thickness and type of plastic you are using. You can repeatedly heat and shape plastic to achieve the desired results, but overheating can damage the surface of the plastic.

TOOLS AND MATERIALS

FORMING TOOL

HEATPROOF TONGS

RUBBER GLOVES

PLASTIC SHEET

HEATPROOF BLOCK OR TRAY

STEEL BLOCK

DOMING BLOCK

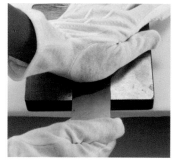

Thermoplastics can be heated and formed into a variety of different shapes.

BASIC TECHNIQUE

1 PREPARATION
Prepare the plastic you will be using by removing all protective material and cleaning off any dust as it can damage the surface. Pre-heat the oven to 180°C (350°F) and arrange your forming tools, tongs, and gloves close to where you will be working. Before you begin you will need to cut and file some extra shapes to use as test pieces: cut several versions of the shape you will be forming.

2 HEATING THE PLASTIC
Wearing protective gloves, place the sheet on a heatproof block or a tray and put it into the oven for about two minutes. The time will depend on the thickness of the sheet you are using. You will know when the sheet is ready if it bends easily when lifted from the tray. Check the plastic every thirty seconds to ensure that it does not become overheated. (If the surface begins to bubble and change colour, it has been heated too much.)

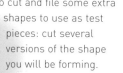

3 SHAPING THE PLASTIC
Still wearing the protective, heatproof gloves, remove the plastic from the oven. It should be soft and flexible. Try making a right angle by pressing the plastic over a steel block or any form that has a sharp-angled edge. It will harden very quickly, so you need to be quick.

Tip
Carry out several experiments before forming the final design. A round bowl is an excellent former for pressing domes.

DOMES

1 CUT OUT A CIRCLE
For a domed shape, cut a circle a little smaller than the form on the doming block that it will be pressed into. You may need a few circles the same size to experiment with.

2 PRESS INTO THE DOME FORM
Heat the circle of plastic as described in Steps 1 and 2, opposite, and press it into the dome form. If the shape is not correct, reheat it and shape it again.

BENDING RODS

1 PREPARATION
Place the rod on a heatproof block or tray and heat it in the oven until it becomes soft and flexible. Rods will take longer than sheet plastic to heat. Once the rod reaches the correct temperature, it will be flexible.

2 SHAPING AROUND A FORM
Hold the rod by the ends and shape it around a round form such as a glass or a mandrel. The rod will cool down very quickly so you will need to be quick.

3 HOLD IN POSITION
Bring the ends together and hold for thirty seconds until the plastic is hard and keeps its shape.

FUSED RINGS
Strips of plastic have been stitched with a sewing machine before being fused together in the oven.

FUSING STRIPS

Wrap strips of flexible plastic around an ovenproof form such as a steel ring mandrel and place in the oven for about three minutes until the plastics melt together. If the strips have not fused together, place the ring mandrel back in the oven for a few minutes longer.

SCREEN PRINTING ON PLASTIC

ANY PATTERN CAN BE PRINTED ON A SHEET OF PLASTIC AND, ONCE PRINTED, THE SHEET CAN BE MADE INTO A PIECE OF JEWELLERY.

Screen printing on plastic can be achieved through the same process as printing on any other material, but you do need to use an ink designed for the plastic you are using. The appropriate ink will create a permanent bond with the plastic and cannot be rubbed off.

Plastic inks tend to be very smooth in consistency and require a fine mesh size to be stretched across the screen. As the mesh is very fine it can become blocked easily, so it is important to clean the screen immediately after use. You will need a special screen wash to dissolve the ink from the mesh.

In general, inks for plastics can be used as they are sold and do not always require a binder. Each type of ink will have specific mixing instructions, so check the manufacturer's advice for the ink you are using. You may choose to add a thinner to the ink before use to increase the spread and prevent the screen from getting blocked. (See page 106 for more on screen printing.)

TOOLS AND MATERIALS

PLASTIC SHEET

SOFT CLOTH

SPARE PAPER

SCREEN

PRINTING TECHNIQUE

FINISHED PRINTS
Here you can see the finished prints alongside the photocopy that was originally exposed to make the screen.

PREPARATION
Before printing, clean the plastic sheet with a soft cloth to remove any dust particles. Lay spare paper on the work surface and place the plastic sheet on top. In this example, an image has been exposed onto the screen. (See pages 106–107 for detailed instructions on screen printing.)

THE PRINTED PLASTIC
In this example, a magenta pattern has been printed onto a solid white sheet of plastic.

THE PRINTED EFFECT ON DIFFERENT PLASTIC
The same design printed on an opaque sheet of plastic; the results are very different compared to the print on the white sheet of plastic.

VACUUM FORMING

VACUUM FORMING IS A PROCESS THAT USES A SPECIALIST MACHINE TO HEAT AND STRETCH A PLASTIC SHEET OVER A MOULD. WHEN THE PLASTIC COOLS, THE MOULDED SHAPE BECOMES PERMANENT AND CAN BE USED TO MAKE A FINAL PIECE OF JEWELLERY OR FOR CASTING. YOU CAN APPLY A PATTERN TO THE PLASTIC WITH INK, PRIOR TO VACUUM FORMING, TO CREATE EFFECTIVE DESIGNS.

A vacuum former is used to heat a sheet of plastic. The machine then stretches the plastic over a mould and uses a vacuum to hold the plastic firmly against the mould. The mould may be made of any firm material such as wood, plaster, plastic or metal. It is important that the sides of the mould are tapered by at least three degrees so that it can be released from the plastic. The mould can have many cavities, but if there are undercuts, it will not release from the plastic, although if you do not need to reuse the mould, you may be able to break it away.

High impact polystyrene (HIPS) is the ideal plastic to use for vacuum forming. The sheet is usually between 1mm ($\frac{1}{32}$in) and 3mm ($\frac{1}{16}$in) thick; thinner sheets will produce more defined shapes. The mould should be relatively shallow in depth to accommodate the stretching capacity of the plastic. The excess plastic can be cut away from the formed piece and used to make a piece of jewellery.

TOOLS AND MATERIALS

VACUUM FORMER

POLYSTYRENE PLASTIC

MOULD FOR FORMING

FORMED RING
by Lesley Strickland
This ring is decorated with formed plastic discs shaped into concave bowls.

BASIC VACUUM FORMING

1 PLACING THE MOULD
Place the mould in the middle of the vacuum-former bed. Lower the former bed to accommodate the plastic sheet.

2 PLACING THE PLASTIC
Lift the clamp and place the plastic over the former bed. The plastic must be slightly larger than the clamp and will rest on the frame above the mould. The plastic sheet used here was screen printed before being vacuum formed (see page 60).

4 HEATING THE PLASTIC

Pull the overhead heater down to cover the plastic. The heating time will depend on the thickness of the plastic and the temperature of the vacuum former, so do some tests before using the final piece. When you think the plastic is ready, push back the overhead heater and check the plastic.

3 CLAMPING THE PLASTIC

Pull the clamp over the plastic and secure it.

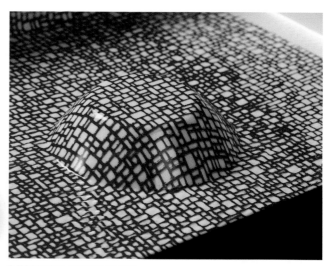

5 FORMING THE PLASTIC

With the overhead heater stowed, use the lever to raise the former bed so that the mould is pressed into the plastic. At the same time, apply air to suck the plastic onto the former bed and firmly over the mould. The plastic will then cool and become rigid within seconds.

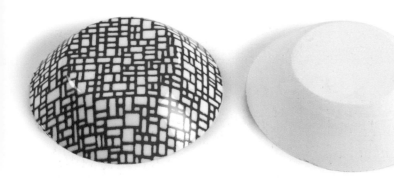

THE FINISHED PIECE

The excess plastic has been trimmed away with a bandsaw. The piece shown here will become a brooch.

USING FOUND OBJECTS

1 CHOOSING OBJECTS
Many kinds of objects can be vacuum formed – such as these chain links – but the sides must be tapered so that you can release them from the moulded plastic.

2 HEATING AND FORMING
Heat and form the plastic as described previously.

Tip
Make several tests to judge the correct amount of heat needed to form the plastic before you begin. It is important not to apply so much heat that the plastic melts, and thinner sheets will require less heat.

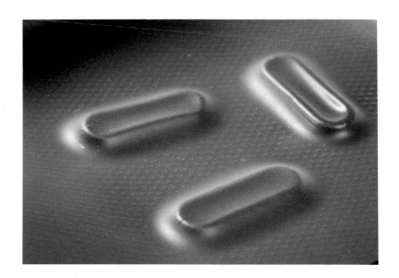

FINISHED BROOCH
Here, the vacuum formed plastic has been mounted onto a silver base and made into a brooch.

THE FINISHED PIECES
The finished plastic will be used as a mould for resin casting (see page 136).

DYEING PLASTIC

DYE IS A POWDERED SUBSTANCE THAT CHANGES THE COLOUR OF THE ITEMS TO WHICH IT'S APPLIED. PIECES TO BE DYED ARE SUBMERGED IN A DYEBATH MADE OF HOT WATER AND THE POWERED DYE.

Dyeing can be used to change the colour of plastic. The process begins with either a transparent or coloured piece of plastic that is submerged in a hot dyebath. Pieces of any size or shape are placed in the bath for a period of time until the colour is absorbed. On plastic, dye is not permanent; it only penetrates the top layer of the plastic and can be removed by sanding. Dyeing should be done during the finishing stages of a piece (with the exception of pieces that are to be heat formed).

TOOLS AND MATERIALS

LARGE HEATPROOF PAN

SMALL SPOON

DISPERSE DYE

HEATPROOF GLOVES

TONGS

PLASTIC RODS AND BUTTONS

BASIC DYEING TECHNIQUE

2 PLACING THE PLASTIC IN THE DYEBATH
Wearing a pair of heatproof gloves and using a pair of tongs, carefully place the plastic, in this example a clear plastic rod, into the boiling dyebath. Boil until the plastic begins to change colour. This may take five to ten minutes.

3 DYEING SMALL PLASTIC PIECES
If you want to dye a number of smaller pieces, such as plastic buttons, it's a good idea to tie them together inside a piece of fabric before placing them in the dyebath; alternatively, place them in a fabric bag.

4 REMOVING PIECES FROM THE BATH
Wear heatproof gloves and use tongs to carefully remove the pieces from the dyebath. The pieces below have just been removed from the dyebath. Wash them under running water to remove any dye particles. Pieces can be returned to the dyebath and boiled for longer if they have not changed colour.

1 MAKING THE DYEBATH
Half-fill a large heatproof pan with water and use a small spoon to add some dye to the water. Follow the instructions provided with the dye you are using for the correct mixing proportions. Bring the water to the boil.

Tips
• *A concentrated dyebath will produce more vibrant colours.*
• *A dyebath tends to be opaque and it may be difficult to see into, so tie strings to your pieces for easy removal.*

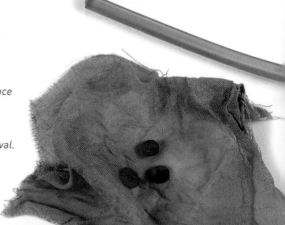

The hot liquid may soften and alter the shape of some pieces, making it necessary to shape them after dyeing.

Disperse dye is a type of dye usually used for dyeing synthetic fabrics, but it can also be used for dyeing plastics. Choosing the correct dye is important because the wrong dye may produce poor results.

There are many types of plastic, and each manufacturer uses a slightly different chemical composition, making it difficult to accurately predict results. There are many variables that affect the dyeing process, including the temperature of the water, the differences between batches of dye, the type of plastic and the length of time the pieces are in the bath. It's a good idea to do a number of samples to get the result you want; several buttons may be dyed in the same dyebath, but when they are removed from the bath, each is a different shade, from vibrant to dull or pale.

DYEING SAMPLES

TWO-TONE EFFECTS

Interesting effects can be achieved when dyeing coloured plastic. The bottom rod shows the colour of the plastic before dyeing. The middle rod was dyed with fuchsia dye, giving a purple tinge, and the rod at the top was dyed orange, making the originally blue rod greenish.

USING DIFFERENT PLASTICS

All of these plastic pieces were placed in the same dyebath but, because they were made of different plastics, different colours have appeared as a result.

FINISHED EARRING

This plastic rod was cut and the hole drilled through the centre before it was dyed.

HEAT-FORMED PIECE

This clear plastic rod was dyed orange before being heat formed. (see page 58).

BANGLES
by Marlene McKibbin

These bangles were heat formed and dyed, creating beautiful translucent colours.

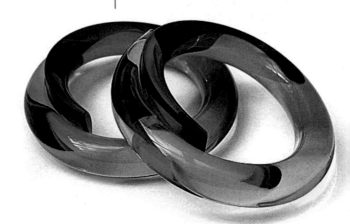

CUTTING AND FOLDING RUBBER

RUBBER IS GENERALLY THOUGHT OF AS AN INDUSTRIAL MATERIAL, AND IT CAN BE UNEXPECTED TO SEE IT IN JEWELLERY DESIGN. IT IS PRECISELY THIS QUALITY THAT MAKES IT AN INTERESTING CHOICE FOR JEWELLERY MAKING.

Rubber is sold in sheets, tubes and rods in a wide range of colours. Patterns can be cut from rubber sheets to be made into earrings, pendants and bracelets. Strips can be cut and folded into interesting shapes or threaded onto a wire or needle. Metal or other solid materials can be inlaid in rods or very thick rubber sheets. Rubber can be drilled, and you can cut slots in it with a sharp knife, into which pieces to be inlaid are inserted and secured with glue.

TOOLS AND MATERIALS

RUBBER SHEET

PEN

PAPER

SCISSORS

CUTTING MAT

KNIFE

METAL RULER

HEAVY-DUTY NEEDLE

STRONG THREAD

HOLE PUNCH

WIRE

RUBBER ROD

DRILL

ALL-PURPOSE GLUE

WIRE CUTTERS

FLAT FILE

RIVETING HAMMER

STEEL BLOCK

USING RUBBER SHEET

1 TRANSFERRING A DESIGN
Use a pen to draw a design onto rubber sheet. It may help if you first cut the design out of paper and trace around it.

2 CUTTING OUT RUBBER
Place the rubber sheet on a cutting mat and use a sharp knife to cut out your design. Apply a fair amount of pressure when cutting thick rubber – you may need to cut the same piece a few times to get through. You can cut a thin rubber sheet with scissors. Experiment on some spare rubber before cutting your design so that you know what will work.

THE FINISHED PIECE
For this necklace, a long strip of rubber was cut into a butterfly design.

Industrial rubber has a slightly sticky surface and will pick up dust. Finished designs can be rubbed with a clean soft cloth to remove any dust and dirt or with an extra fine steel wool for a matt finish.

Tip
Any visible pen marks can be removed by rubbing with a cloth.

NECKLACE
by Thea Tolsma
This rubber necklace has an intricate plant design cut into it.

THREADING FOLDED RUBBER LOOPS

1 CUTTING RUBBER STRIPS
Place a sheet of rubber on a cutting mat. Lay a metal ruler on the rubber and use a sharp knife to cut against the edge of the ruler. For thick rubber, you may need to make a second cut without moving the ruler.

2 PIERCING THE RUBBER STRIPS
To pierce holes into your strips of rubber sheet, use a heavy-duty needle with a strong thread. Pierce the rubber and slide it along the needle. Alternatively, you could first make holes along the length of the rubber with a heavy-duty hole punch (see page 77) and thread it onto a length of wire. Choose the method that best suits your design.

3 FOLDING THE RUBBER STRIPS
Make a loop in the rubber strips and thread it onto the needle. The loop can be made to any size; each loop can be different. Some experimentation will be necessary to find the method that works best for your design.

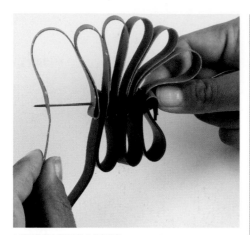

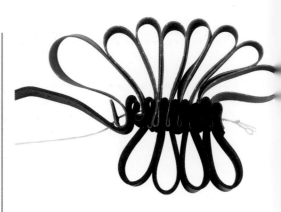

4 THREADING LOOPS

Continue threading loops onto the needle until the needle is full.

5 PULLING ONTO THE THREAD

Hold the loops and pull the needle through so that the rubber slides onto the thread. Continue threading until all the lengths of rubber have been used up.

6 MAKING A PIECE OF JEWELLERY

This technique lends itself well to making a necklace and bracelet. This sample shows the beginning of a bracelet.

HOOPED EARRINGS
by Min-Ji Cho

To make these earrings, black rubber gloves were cut up and folded and are held together with silver wire.

PEARL AND RUBBER NECKLACE
by Min-Ji Cho

This necklace was made by stringing together pearls and the tips of pink rubber gloves.

WIRE INLAID RUBBER BRACELET

Rubber rods 4mm (⅛in) or thicker can be used for making bracelets. A craft knife can cut up to 6mm (¼in) rods as shown in this example. Silver wire or tubes can be inlaid into the rubber rod for decoration.

1 CUTTING THE ROD
Take a length of rubber rod and place it on a cutting mat. Using a sharp knife, cut it to the length you need to make a bracelet.

2 A HOLE FOR A METAL ROD
The bracelet is to have pieces of wire inlaid into it, so drill or cut a hole in the rubber the same size as the metal to be inserted. Apply a small amount of strong all-purpose glue to the metal and then insert the wire into the hole and push until you can feel it on the other side. Cut the spare wire with a pair of wire cutters leaving 1mm (¹⁄₃₂in) sticking out.

3 FILING THE INLAID WIRE FLAT
Use a flat file to file the wire flush with the surface of the rubber rod. Be careful not to file the rubber.

4 RIVETING THE WIRE
For extra security, place the rubber on a steel block and use a riveting hammer to smooth both ends of the wire. (Omit this step if the piece is glued securely in the rubber.)

THE FINISHED PIECE
The finished piece can be made into a bracelet by gluing the end of the rod inside a silver lube.

DIAMONDS AND RUBBER
by Andre Ribeiro
There is a striking visual contrast between the diamonds and the black matt rubber rods used in these pieces.

CHAPTER 3

FABRIC, FIBRES AND LEATHER

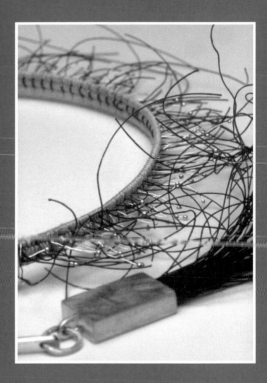

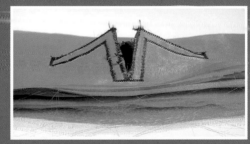

NECKLACE *(opposite)*
by Silvina Romero
Scrap fabric and thread were
combined to make this necklace

NECKLACE *(left)*
by Vannetta Seecharran
Necklace combining woven
red threads and silver.

BANGLE *(top right)*
by Tomasz Donocik
Men's bangle made with
gold and leather.

BRACELET *(bottom right)*
by Vannetta Seecharran
This bracelet is made entirely
from fabric and thread.

This chapter demonstrates how traditional textile and
leather techniques such as skiving, stitching, weaving,
crochet and knotting, and other more unusual techniques,
such as flocking, can be used for jewellery making. Many
of the techniques are very simple and can be successfully
carried out by a beginner.

FABRIC, FIBRE AND LEATHER PROPERTIES

'ALTERNATIVE' MATERIALS ARE VERY POPULAR FOR USE IN CONTEMPORARY JEWELLERY MAKING, AND MORE AND MORE JEWELLERS ARE BORROWING TECHNIQUES SUCH AS SEWING, CROCHETING AND FLOCKING FROM OTHER CRAFT DISCIPLINES.

FABRIC: There is a wide range of fabrics available, from natural to synthetic in numerous finishes, colours, textures and patterns. Fabrics can be manipulated by cutting, folding and heat-shaping, and patterns can be printed onto them to create interesting effects. One of the difficulties of using fabric is using it in combination with metal; you will need to employ clever joining methods to make for a comfortable visual and practical connection.

COTTON AND METALLIC FIBRES

BEADS

WOOL FIBRES

FIBRE: A fibre is a strand or thread of material made into yarn. Natural fibres include cotton, silk and wool, while synthetic fibres are made from a range of chemical compositions. Fibres are traditionally used by textile designers; however, they can be used to make jewellery through crocheting, knotting, stringing beads and weaving. Synthetic fibres tend to be stronger and can carry more weight than natural fibres, but they are both available in a selection of colours.

LEATHER: Leather is created through the tanning of hides and skins of animals, and during the tanning process the skins are made durable and suitable for working. Skins are available in varying thicknesses and can be cut, stitched and glued to create jewellery pieces. Heavier leather lends itself to making simple patterns and should be cut with a very sharp knife. Thinner leather can be cut with a pair of sharp scissors. Leather may be decorated by hand or machine stitched and can be glued together to form a strong bond.

DESIGNING WITH FABRIC, FIBRES AND LEATHER

Qualities Soft, colourful, textured, synthetic or natural, lacking in rigid structure.

Applications Fabric is soft and lightweight and can be cut, sewn and given structure through heat manipulation. Larger pieces of fabric can be pleated to create necklaces and bracelets.

Fibres can be crocheted, knitted and knotted to create jewellery pieces. Strands can be twisted together to create cords on which to hang pendants.

Leather can be cut, glued and stitched. It can be moulded and patterned. It can be made thinner, and pieces can be glued together to increase thickness. Strips of leather make excellent straps for necklaces and bracelets, and skins can be folded to create shapes.

Combining with other materials Fabric, fibres and leather are available in a vast range of colours and can be combined with most materials but work particularly well when combined with metal. Methods of connecting metal to fabric, fibres and leather include riveting, stitching and gluing.

Where to look for inspiration Take a look at the websites below for inspiration from jewellers working with fabric, fibres and leather.
• **Natalya Pinchuk, United States**
www.natalyapinchuk.com
Wool, enamel and plastics, large-scale tactile jewellery.
• **Felike Van der Leest, Netherlands**
www.feliekevanderleest.com
Crochet and mixed media, whimsical animal pieces.
• **Uli Rapp, Netherlands**
www.uli.nu
Screen-printed leather jewellery, a surreal use of traditional jewellery imagery.

LEATHER

SILK FIBRES

CUTTING LEATHER

LEATHER CAN BE CUT INTO A VARIETY OF DIFFERENT SHAPES WITH A KNIFE, A LASER CUTTER OR SCISSORS. THESE PIECES CAN THEN BE INCORPORATED INTO JEWELLERY.

Other than a laser cutter, using a knife is probably the simplest way of cutting leather. A knife for cutting leather must have a strong blade and be able to cut through thick skins. Ordinary craft knives can work on thin skins but may not work as well on thicker skins. Scissors can also be used on thinner skins; however, the edges of the cut leather may not be as clean as when cut with a knife. If you're confident, you can draw designs directly onto the leather using a pen or chalk but it's a good idea to cut designs out in paper first to make a template, and then draw around the template onto the leather.

TOOLS AND MATERIALS

LEATHER

CUTTING MAT

RULER

KNIFE/SCISSORS

PEN

PUNCH

RAWHIDE MALLET

LEATHER BRACELET
by Jane Willingale
This leather bracelet was constructed using two different colours of leather, the separate parts riveted together.

BASIC CUTTING TECHNIQUE

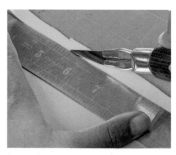

1 CUTTING STRIPS OF LEATHER
Lay the leather on a cutting mat. Place the ruler on the leather and hold firmly in position. Applying pressure, run the blade along the edge of the ruler. Try to cut the leather in the first pull to get a clean edge; however, thicker skins may require a second pull. You can also cut freehand but this may take some practice.

2 DRAWING A DESIGN ONTO LEATHER
Using a ballpoint pen, draw your design onto the back of the leather either by tracing around a template or drawing freehand.

3 CUTTING WITH SCISSORS
Use a pair of sharp scissors and cut around the drawn line.

Tip
To cut curved leather shapes, make a template out of cardboard and use the edge as a guide for cutting.

4 MAKING HOLES
Lay the leather on a cutting mat and mark the place where you would like to make a hole. Place the punch on the leather and use a rawhide mallet to hammer the head of the punch. Any punch that is sharp enough to cut leather can be used. Here, a punch specially designed for leather is used.

STITCHING AND EDGING

LEATHER IS GENERALLY STITCHED WITH AN INDUSTRIAL SEWING MACHINE; HOWEVER, THIN PIECES OF LEATHER CAN BE STITCHED BY HAND OR WITH A DOMESTIC SEWING MACHINE.

Thick skins must be stitched with a machine appropriate for leather. Such a machine has a special foot that allows the leather to be stitched smoothly. Thinner skins can be stitched with a domestic sewing machine and need only a special leather needle and a machine foot made of nylon. A leather needle has a slightly different point to pierce through the skin. Skins can also be stitched by hand using premade holes. An awl, a sharp tool used for making a hole, is used for making holes in leather and a wax-coated thread is used for stitching.

TOOLS AND MATERIALS
PIECES OF LEATHER
COTTON THREAD
SEWING MACHINE
GLUE
SMALL BRUSH
ACRYLIC-BASED INK
DAMP CLOTH

EDGING

A freshly cut edge can look messy and frayed. To keep this from happening, an acrylic-based dye can be applied to the edge with a small brush. You can also use an edging tool – a plastic tool with grooves – to rub along the edge and make it smooth after dyeing. The dye can be used to highlight an edge by applying a contrasting colour to that of the leather, and this can make an attractive feature.

LEATHER LEAF EARRINGS
by Tanya Igic
These leaf-shaped leather and silver earrings were made using layered leather.

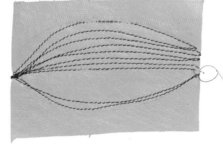

MACHINE STITCHING
This example was stitched using a domestic machine and cotton thread. This thin piece of leather will be glued onto another piece to increase the thickness. (See page 76.)

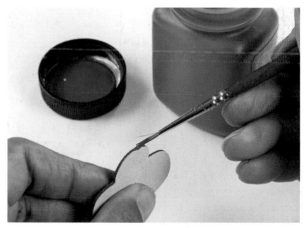

APPLYING EDGING COLOUR
Use a small brush to apply a thin coat of ink to the edge of the leather. The ink may smear onto the surface of the leather, but it can be wiped off with a damp cloth while it is wet. Once the ink dries it is more difficult to remove.

GLUING AND SKIVING

TWO PIECES OF LEATHER CAN BE GLUED TOGETHER WITH CONTACT CEMENT OR STRONG BONDING GLUE APPLIED TO BOTH PIECES AND PRESSED TOGETHER. LEATHER CAN BE MADE THINNER WITH A KNIFE CALLED A SKIVING KNIFE.

Contact cement is a clear-drying flexible acrylic adhesive that is used on plastic, rubber, leather and wood. The glue is applied to both surfaces, then left to dry for ten minutes; the surfaces are then pressed together and need a further thirty minutes to dry completely. The glue has a strong smell and should be used in a ventilated area.

Finished pieces can be glued together, or the skins can be glued and then cut once they are dry. Pieces can be glued together to increase the thickness of a skin, or two different colours may be glued to make a reversible piece.

Skiving is a process of making leather thinner; it is particularly useful for thinning seams that will be folded. Skiving knives are very sharp; on some knives the blade is flat with a rounded or pointed tip, while others have a curved blade. There is a huge range of skiving knives available, so check with your leather supplier to find out the best kind to use.

FUCHSIA NECKLACE
by Tanya Igic
This necklace was made from layered leather and silver.

TOOLS AND MATERIALS

BRUSH

CONTACT-CEMENT GLUE

LEATHER

BONE FOLDER

SKIVING KNIFE

GLUING

1 APPLYING GLUE
Use a brush with firm bristles to apply a thin layer of glue to the back of both pieces of leather. Leave them for ten minutes so they are touch-dry.

2 PUTTING THE PIECES TOGETHER
Place one piece on top of the other and rub down to flatten. Pulling the leather apart once it is glued can be very difficult, so if you make a mistake, you may need to start again.

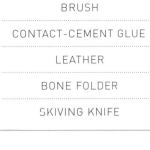

SKIVING

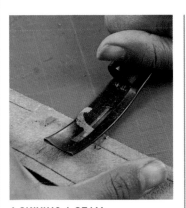

1 SKIVING A SEAM
When skiving a seam, draw a line on the back of the leather to guide the knife. Place the skiving knife on the leather and pull towards you applying an even pressure. Too much pressure will cut through the leather. Practise on some spare leather before attempting a final piece.

2 GLUING SKIVED EDGES
Apply a thin layer of glue on the back of the skived seam. Allow ten minutes for the glue to dry before folding over the edge. Rub over the edge with a bone folder or another tool with a smooth tip to secure it.

RIVETS AND EYELETS

RIVETS AND EYELETS CAN BE SET INTO PREDRILLED HOLES IN LEATHER. THEY ARE ESSENTIAL FINDINGS FOR MAKING LEATHER JEWELLERY AND CAN BE USED TO CONNECT PIECES OF LEATHER TOGETHER.

A rivet is a two-part mechanical fastener that has a shaft on one end. Rivets are set in predrilled holes; one shaft fits inside the other, and they are hammered to secure them. Rivets are used to connect two pieces of material together, and some allow movement between the riveted pieces.

An eyelet is a metal ring that serves as a reinforcement to a hole in leather, paper or fabric. Eyelets are set in premade holes, and a variety of tools and machines can be used for setting them. The easiest way to set an eyelet is to use a hand-setting tool that includes a punch and a base. Eyelets reinforce a hole that may be under strain or is used often.

RIVETS

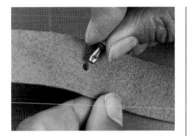

1 PLACING THE BOTTOM RIVET
Punch a hole to fit the size of rivet you are using, turn the piece so the back is facing up and insert the bottom rivet through the hole.

2 PLACING THE TOP RIVET
Turn the piece around so the front is facing up. Lay it on a firm surface and place any additional pieces to be held in place by the rivet. Insert the top rivet into the bottom rivet.

3 SECURING THE RIVET
Use a mallet to tap the head of the top rivet lightly to secure it on the bottom rivet.

TOOLS AND MATERIALS
HOLE PUNCH
RIVETS
HAMMER
EYELETS
EYELET FIXING TOOL
PUNCH
RAWHIDE MALLET

EYELETS

1 PLACING THE EYELET IN THE FIXING TOOL
Punch a hole in the leather to fit the eyelet. Place the eyelet inside the cavity of the fixing tool. Place the hole over the eyelet. (Follow the instructions for the particular eyelet tool you are using.)

2 SECURING THE EYELET
Place the punch over the eyelet and tap the head of the punch with a mallet. The edges of the eyelet should spread out and flatten, securing it in the leather.

BUCKLES AND OTHER FIXTURES

BUCKLES INTENDED FOR LEATHER SHOES AND BAGS CAN ALSO BE USED TO FINISH JEWELLERY PIECES. THEY CAN BE USED AS CLASPS OR AS A DESIGN FEATURE.

Findings such as buckles, hooks and rings can all be used for finishing leather jewellery. There are also commercially available silver findings that are made especially for leather. The choice you make depends on the finish you are looking for and the type of piece it will be used on. Shoe and bag findings tend to be chunky and industrial, whereas silver findings are smaller. Most findings are glued directly onto the leather; however, some are riveted.

The metal findings you use on leather can also be used on fabric and ribbons, but fabric ends will need to be secured by stitching first to prevent fraying and to keep the metal findings from falling off.

BRASS OVAL RING

This is a common type of ring used on bag handles. You can use it on a necklace to connect two different types of leather and to give an 'industrial' look to a piece.

STEEL BUCKLE

This type of buckle is used on bags and can also be used to secure a bracelet.

SHOE BUCKLE

Shoe buckles are small enough to work well on leather bracelets.

RECTANGULAR END CAP

This hollow end cap is made for flat leather strips. The leather is secured by gluing it in place.

END CAP WITH TEETH

This type of end cap has teeth inside that are squeezed shut over the material. It may be used with leather or ribbons.

LARGE ROUNDED END CAP

These large rounded end caps are attached to the leather with epoxy glue.

ROUNDED END CAP

This rounded end cap is used on the end of a leather or fabric cord and is glued with a strong glue.

SMALL RECTANGULAR END CAP

This small rectangular end cap is ideal for use with slender, flat pieces of leather thong.

SMALL ROUNDED END CAP

This small rounded end cap works well on fabric or thin leather cords.

STRINGING

BEADS AND BUTTONS AND OTHER SMALL OBJECTS CAN BE STRUNG TOGETHER TO MAKE A PIECE OF JEWELLERY. THE GENERAL PRINCIPLE OF STRINGING IS TO START WITH BEADING WIRE, SECURE ONE END WITH A CRIMP BEAD AND JUMP RING, AND THREAD FROM THE OTHER END. BEADS, BUTTONS, PLASTIC TOYS, STONES, SEEDS OR ANYTHING THAT HAS A HOLE CAN BE STRUNG. THE ONLY ESSENTIAL REQUIREMENT IS FOR THE HOLE TO BE BIG ENOUGH TO FIT ON THE BEADING WIRE YOU ARE USING.

Some of the most common beading wires include nylon wire, nylon-coated steel wire, and beading thread; however, any strong string can be used that fits the holes of the beads you are using.

Beading threads can be silk, cotton or synthetic and are suitable for stringing large beads. Nylon wire is thin, transparent, flexible wire that is ideal for intricate beadwork or for stringing small beads. Nylon-coated steel wire is very strong and is made up of lots of strands of steel wire twisted together. It can be used for a variety of stringing jobs, including single strand, multistrand and invisible designs. All beading wires are available in a range of sizes ranging from very fine to thick.

TOOLS AND MATERIALS

WIRE

METAL RULER

WIRE CUTTERS

CRIMPING PLIERS

CRIMPS

JUMP RING

CRIMP COVERS

CALOTTES

NEEDLE-NOSE PLIERS

COTTON CORD

CLASPS

BEADS

TASSELS

Tip
Thicker wire tends to kink and is most suitable for heavy beads – the weight of the beads evens out any kinks.

CRIMPS

Crimp beads are tube-shaped metal beads that require special pliers, known as crimping pliers (see page 10), to secure them on the beading wire. Crimp beads are available in a range of sizes – use the correct crimp for the size of your wire. If the wrong crimp is used, the piece can break loose and fall apart.

Crimp beads can be hidden with a crimp cover, an open metal bead placed over the crimp bead and closed with a pair of pliers.

Before stringing, secure one end of the beading wire with a soldered jump ring and a crimp bead. Once the wire is filled with beads, another soldered jump ring and crimp bead are used to

secure the other end. Both ends will have a soldered jump ring, and these can be connected with a clasp.

Another type of crimp bead is a calotte, which is used in place of a soldered jump ring at the ends of a beading wire. Beading wire can also be attached directly to a jump ring.

CRIMPING

1 MEASURING
Measure out the length of wire you need for your design and add 10cm (4in). Use a pair of wire cutters to cut the length of wire.

2 STARTING OFF
Thread a crimp bead and a soldered jump ring onto the beading wire. Be sure that the jump ring is closed because the wire will pull through any gap. This method of starting can be applied to most beading thread as well as wire.

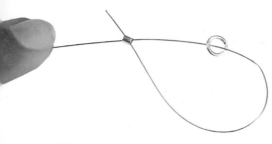

3 HOLDING THE WIRE

Pass the end of the wire into the crimp bead. The jump ring should be sitting in the loop. Next, hold both pieces of wire and push the crimp bead close to the jump ring.

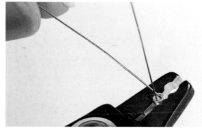

4 CRIMPING THE WIRE

Use a pair of crimping pliers and place the crimp bead inside the back notch, away from the tip of the pliers. The crimp bead should fit comfortably in the groove for accurate crimping.

5 SQUEEZING THE CRIMP

Squeeze the handle of the crimping pliers to make a dent in the middle of the crimp bead. Remove the pliers – the bead should have a dent in the middle.

6 FOLDING THE CRIMP OVER

Place the crimp bead standing up in the front notch of the crimping pliers so the dent is facing out. Squeeze the handle of the pliers to fold the crimp in half.

7 APPLYING THE CRIMP COVER

Hold the crimp cover inside the front notches of the crimping pliers. Place the crimp bead inside the crimp cover. Gently squeeze the handle of the crimping pliers to close the cover. The crimp cover should remain round and have the appearance of a bead.

8 CALOTTE

A calotte is two half-spheres with a loop attached to the top. The end of the beading wire is secured inside the calotte and a jump ring and clasp are attached to the loop. The wire can then be strung with beads. Thread a crimp onto the end of the beading wire and crimp. Position a calotte around the crimp and use a pair of crimping or needle-nose pliers to close the calotte so that it remains in place.

9 USING BEADING CORD

Calottes can also be used with cotton cord. Knot the end of the cord and place it inside the calotte. Use a pair of crimping or needle-nose pliers to close the crimp. The crimp should remain round once it is closed.

10 CRIMPING WITH A CLASP

Some commercially available clasps have a loop on one end that can be used for threading the beading wire. In this case, the beaded wire can be placed inside the loop and crimped as described in Steps 4, 5 and 6.

FINISHED PIECE

The ends of this piece are secured with a calotte. A jump ring is attached to both ends with a clasp. The beads are held apart with knots (see page 84).

3 REMOVING GAPS

Hold the jump ring and pull the short end of the wire – keeping the crimp near the bead – until there are no visible gaps. Crimp the end of the wire as described in Crimping Steps 4 to 7.

SINGLE-STRAND BEADING

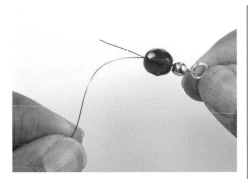

1 STARTING OFF

Choose beading wire to fit the beads you are using. Measure, cut and crimp the wire as described in Crimping Steps 1 to 7. Using a tape measure or string, find the correct length before cutting the wire and add around 10cm (4in) to the length to allow for crimping. Thread the first bead onto the beading wire and hide the short end of the wire inside the first few beads. Thread the beads to fill the wire.

2 ENDING CRIMP

Check that the length of the wire is correct by holding the piece to your body and adjust it by cutting off any extra length. Thread a crimp and then a soldered jump ring and pass the wire back through the crimp. Push the beads along the strand to remove any spare wire.

4 TRIMMING THE EXTRA WIRE

Trim the extra wire with a pair of wire cutters. The two ends can be connected with a clasp.

FINISHED PIECE

The finished piece will have a clasp attached to it.

▶

STRINGING A TASSEL

1 THREADING THE TASSEL

In this example, a tassel forms the central feature of the design. This technique can be used on any length of wire. Select your tassel and choose a bead that has a hole big enough to fit over the top of the tassel. Cut the wire to suit the length of your design. Thread the tassel onto the beading wire.

4 ENDING

Crimp one end as described in Crimping Steps 2 to 7 and repeat for the other end.

5 ATTACHING A CHAIN

Use open jump rings to attach a length of chain to each of the beaded strands you have made.

FINISHED PIECE

The invisible-strand technique can be done with clear nylon thread for a really 'invisible' effect.

INVISIBLE STRAND

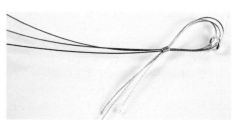

1 STARTING OFF

Cut three strands of beading wire to the same length to suit the area of the body you are designing for. To start, repeat Crimping Steps 1 to 7, page 79. This technique can be done with different numbers of strands.

2 ADDING THE FIRST BEAD

Bring both ends of the wire together and thread the bead. Slide the bead down to cover the top of the tassel.

3 ADDING THE REST OF THE BEADS

Separate the wires and thread the beads, leaving 5cm (2in) at the end for crimping.

FINISHED PIECE

The two ends of the necklace can be connected with a clasp to make a long necklace.

2 THREADING THE FIRST BEAD

Use a bead with a hole big enough to fit all of the strands. Thread the bead and then a crimp, hiding the wire ends in the crimp. Use a pair of needle-nose pliers to flatten the crimp bead and trim any extra wire.

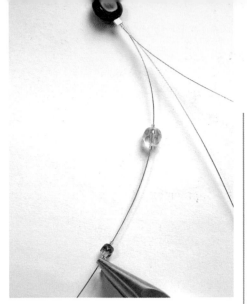

SPLIT STRAND

2 BRINGING THE STRANDS TOGETHER

Bring the strands together and thread a bead onto both. This will join the strands – you can add more than one bead at this stage if you like.

3 SEPARATING THE STRANDS

This technique requires a small crimp bead that can be secured with needle-nose pliers. Separate the three strands and select one. Thread a crimp bead onto the strand about 5cm (2in) from the first bead. Flatten the crimp with a pair of needle-nose pliers. Thread a bead followed by a crimp and flatten – the crimp is to secure the bead in one place. Repeat this step until you reach the end of the strand and leave 5cm (2in) spare wire. Repeat the process on the other strands.

1 STARTING OFF

This technique can be done with many strands of beading wire, but in this example two strands are used. Cut two strands of beading wire to the same length to suit the area you are designing for. Repeat Crimping Steps 2 to 7. Thread one bead onto all the strands. Separate the strands and thread each one to the point where you would like to join them together.

3 FINISHING

The strands can be separated and rejoined several times until you reach the end. Repeat Crimping Steps 2 to 7 to finish off.

4 ENDING

Bring the three ends together and to finish, repeat Crimping Steps 2 to 7. Connect the ends with a clasp.

FINISHED PIECE

The finished bracelet is joined with a clasp.

KNOTTING

FOR JEWELLERY MAKING, KNOTS ARE GENERALLY USED FOR TYING BEADS ALONG A STRAND TO CREATE A DESIGN. SOME KNOTS ARE TIED ON EITHER SIDE OF BEADS TO KEEP THEM IN ONE PLACE ON A CORD; OTHER KNOTS ARE TIED BETWEEN BEADS TO KEEP THEM APART.

Leather cord, cotton beading thread and ribbons can all be knotted, and a number of items can be knotted onto them, including beads, buttons, semi-precious stones, seeds and anything that has a suitable hole.

A piece of knotted jewellery can be started in many ways. An overhand knot can be made at the end of the strand, or a crimp (see page 79) may be used to stop the beads from sliding off. The end of any knotted piece can end in either a tassel or more beads. Tassels give a fun look and are easy to use.

TOOLS AND MATERIALS

BEADING THREAD, CORD OR RIBBON

CRIMP

NEEDLE-NOSE PLIERS

BEADS

BUTTONS

TASSEL

1 STARTING OFF
This technique can be used with any beading thread and is the starting point for a lariat – a necklace that does not have a clasp, but instead ties at the front. First, knot the end of the beading thread, in this case leather cord, and thread on a crimp (see page 79). Flatten the crimp with a pair of needle-nose pliers to keep the beads from sliding off. A crimp provides additional security and is not necessary if the knot is secure. Thread the starting beads that will sit at the end of the strand.

BASIC KNOTTING

2 MAKING AN OVERHAND KNOT
Make a loop on the strand farthest away from the starting bead. Pass the end under and into the loop. Don't pull it tight. Hold the bead and strand and use your fingers to guide the loop close to the top of the bead. Keep the knot loose until it is close to the bead.

3 TIGHTEN THE KNOT
Hold the bead with one hand and hold the strand in the other. Pull the knot tight, as close to the bead as possible.

THE FINISHED PIECE
The finished knotted lariat is decorated with a variety of beads, buttons and roses.

4 KNOTTING A BUTTON

Choose a position on the strand where you would like the button to sit. Make an overhand knot as described in Step 2. Thread the button and move it next to the knot. Pull the cord tight and make another overhand knot close to the button. The technique is exactly the same as for a bead; the button is secured in place by an overhand knot on either side.

5 ADDING A SECOND BUTTON

This time a different style of button is threaded, and the knotting technique is the same as in the previous steps.

THREADING BEADS OVER TASSELS

1 STARTING WITH A TASSEL

For this technique, the necklace does not have a clasp, and the ends hang in front. Threading starts from one end, and a tassel is used to finish the ends. A fabric beading cord is used for threading and is ideal for small beads.

Choose a bead with a hole big enough to fit around the top of the tassel. Thread the bead and leave about 7.5cm (3in) of spare cord. Thread the tassel through the short end.

THE FINISHED PIECE

The finished necklace does not have a clasp and is fastened with a loose knot so that the tassels hang in front.

2 PASSING THE END THROUGH

Take the short end of the thread and pass it through the bottom hole of the bead. Use one hand to push the thread through and the other hand to pull the thread. Holding both threads, pull the bead over the top of the tassel. Secure with a knot and trim the excess thread.

3 KNOTTING ABOVE THE BEAD

The remaining strand can be threaded with beads. You can fill the entire thread with beads or leave gaps between beads by knotting on either side of them.

▶

KNOTTING CORD

KNOT A BEAD TO THE CORD

Thread a bead onto the beading cord and, once it is in position, make an overhand knot.

THE FINISHED PIECE

Make the finished piece into a necklace by tying a clasp on both ends.

KNOTTING WITH RIBBON

1 KNOTTING WITH TWO RIBBONS

Choose a bead with a hole big enough to fit the ribbon. Secure the ends of the ribbon to your work surface with masking tape to make threading easier. Then, make an overhand knot a few inches away from the ends of the ribbons and thread the first bead. Make another knot above the bead.

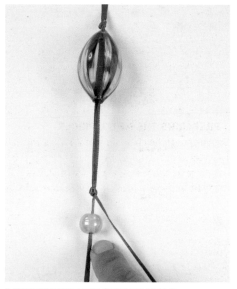

2 THREADING THE SECOND BEAD

Leave some space and make another knot where you would like the next bead to sit. Separate the ribbons and thread a bead through one ribbon.

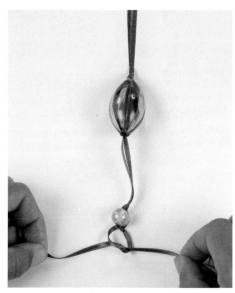

3 KNOTTING AFTER THE BEAD

Take both ribbons – one should be sitting outside the bead – and make an overhand knot, then pull it tight. Make a second knot above the first and pull tight. The bead should feel secure. Repeat these steps until you have the required length of threaded beads.

STITCHING LINKS

STITCHING IS A BASIC TEXTILE TECHNIQUE THAT IS USED BY MANY INDUSTRIES AND TAKES MANY FORMS. THERE ARE MANY TYPES OF STITCHES, SOME DECORATIVE AND OTHERS FUNCTIONAL.

Stitching uses a length of thread to secure two pieces of material together, and it can be done on a sewing machine or by hand. Cotton thread, wire and cord are just a few materials that can be used for stitching. Generally stitches are sewn in a straight line, where one stitch follows the other and each stitch is the same length. However, handstitching can be random, varying in length and size.

Metal can be stitched onto any material by way of a series of drilled holes and the use of a strong thread or wire. When stitching is relied upon for strength, an appropriate thread is required, because some threads will rub against the edge of other materials and will wear over time. A similar technique can be used with other materials, such as leather.

TOOLS AND MATERIALS

DRILL OR PUNCH

SHEET METAL PIECES (OR OTHER MATERIAL TO BE STITCHED)

NEEDLE

THREAD

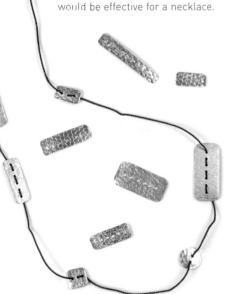

THE FINISHED PIECE
You may choose to leave a gap between the pieces or stitch them close together. This technique would be effective for a necklace.

METAL LINKS

1 PREPARING THE METAL PIECES
Drill or punch holes in the metal pieces you will be threading. The holes can be in a straight line or in a random order, and you can make as many holes as you need for your design.

2 THREADING THE NEEDLE
Choose a thread that is suitable for the pieces you are stitching and a matching needle that will fit through the holes. Thread the needle and pull around 10cm (4in) of the thread through.

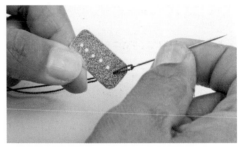

3 MAKING THE FIRST STITCH
Pass the needle through the first hole and pull the length of thread through.

4 STITCHING SUBSEQUENT HOLES
Pass the needle through the second hole and pull the length through. Repeat for the other holes. Continue with the other pieces of sheet metal, until you have stitched all the pieces.

DECORATIVE STITCHING

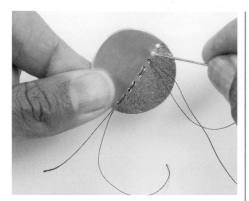

1 DECORATIVE STITCHING

Drill a series of holes in a piece of sheet metal or other material and use a needle to stitch thread through it. The stitching technique is the same as described in Steps 1 to 4 of Metal links.

2 THE FINISHED PIECE

You can leave the ends of the thread long or trim them away with a pair of scissors.

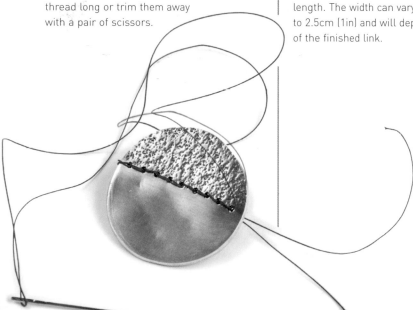

STITCHED FABRIC LINKS

Fabric links can be joined together to make a necklace. Different coloured fabrics can be used for additional interest.

1 CUTTING STRIPS

Measure the finished length of each link. Double the measurement and add 2.5cm (1in). Cut several strips of fabric to this length. The width can vary from 1cm (⅜in) to 2.5cm (1in) and will depend on the width of the finished link.

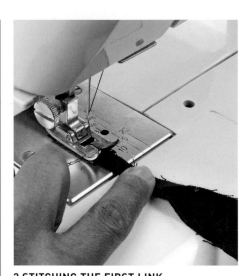

2 STITCHING THE FIRST LINK

Set the machine to a zigzag stitch or a straight stitch. You can either fold the fabric over or stitch it down the middle. Stitch along the entire length of the fabric.

3 BRING THE ENDS TOGETHER

Bring the ends together to form a loop and stitch over the ends to secure them.

4 MAKING A SECOND LINK
Take the second strip of fabric and thread the first link inside. Stitch down the centre of the second link. Bring the ends together and secure them, as you did for the first link.

THE FINISHED PIECE
Repeat this process until you have made the desired number of links in your chain.

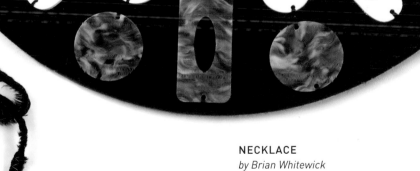

NECKLACE
by Brian Whitewick
In this necklace, pieces of acrylic sheet are stitched to felt. The stitching is both functional and decorative.

WEAVING

WEAVING IS THE PROCESS OF MAKING A LENGTH OF CLOTH FROM TWO SETS OF INTERLOCKING YARNS OR THREADS. THE TWO DIRECTIONS OF THE FIBRES ARE CALLED THE 'WARP', RUNNING LENGTHWAYS, AND THE 'WEFT', WHICH RUNS ACROSS.

Weaving is traditionally done on a loom. The warp threads are fixed in position and alternate threads are separated by a foot pedal to allow the weft thread to pass between them from one side to the other. For jewellery making, handweaving is the simplest method to use. The techniques for handweaving are the same as those used on a loom, except the warp threads will need to be secured somehow to enable you to weave the weft back and forth with ease. In the example below, the warp threads are held in position by a heavy steel block.

WEAVING THROUGH METAL STRIPS

TOOLS AND MATERIALS

TAPE OR HEAVY OBJECT

METAL STRIPS

YARN

OTHER OBJECTS

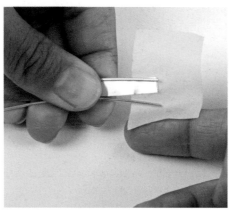

1 SECURING THE WARP
Measure the area you are designing; this measurement will determine the length of the warp. Add extra length to allow you to finish the ends. Secure the ends of the warp, either by taping them down, or in a loom. The warp may be threads, wires or a combination of both and other materials. Here, metal strips have been used; however, the same principle applies to other materials and for handmade looms.

2 STARTING WEAVING
Leave a few inches of yarn at one end. Pass the rest under the first strip then over the second and under the third. Repeat this pattern of over and under until you reach the last strip of the warp.

THE FINISHED PIECES
The finished pieces are fitted with silver end pieces and shaped into necklaces.

A number of materials can be used for the warp and the weft threads, including metal strips or wire. Wire woven into the length of a piece will add structure to the cloth; the wires can be placed strategically either on the warp or weft. Other objects can be woven into the cloth, including beads, yarn or thin strips of metal. If you are using metal strips for the warp, these can be secured at one end with tape, and the weft can be moved across between them.

For the purpose of jewellery making, a loom may not be necessary, but you can make a hand loom very quickly using an old picture frame and a series of nails hammered into all four sides at equal intervals. This is a quick method of making a loom and can be used for weaving threads.

The weaving method in the example shown below is only suitable if you are using metal as the warp.

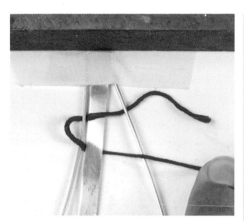

3 RETURNING THE YARN

The next step depends on whether the yarn is under or over the last strip.

If the yarn went under the end strip, pass the yarn back over the end strip and under the next strip and repeat until you reach the side you started from. If the yarn is over the end strip, pass it under that strip and then over the next and repeat to the end.

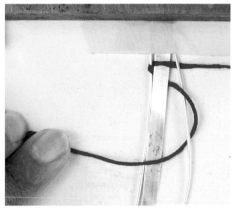

4 CONTINUING WEAVING

Repeat Step 3 and return the yarn to the other side. Repeat Steps 3 and 4 until you have woven the desired length.

5 TIGHTENING THE WEFT

Use your finger to push the yarn so the weft is tight and close together.

WEAVING IN METAL OBJECTS

1 ADD THE OBJECT

Choose the position where you would like to add the shape and thread it into as many warp strips as you choose.

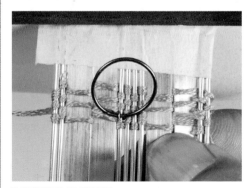

2 MAKING IT TIGHT

Continue weaving the yarn and push the weft threads tightly together.

GLUING

JEWELLERS OFTEN DON'T LIKE TO USE GLUE AND WILL FIND OTHER WAYS OF SECURING TWO PIECES TOGETHER; HOWEVER, GLUING IS SOMETIMES NECESSARY WHEN CONNECTING TWO DIFFERENT MATERIALS, SUCH AS METAL AND FABRIC.

Glue should be used discreetly, so that it is not visible. Generally speaking, glue does not provide structural support, and it is best used on areas that will not be under strain. For the best results, the fabric should be inserted into a slot, where it will be under pressure.

Gluing is only appropriate for securing pieces that cannot be connected in any other way and can be used for a range of materials. You can also use tape to secure loose strands and to provide additional grip for the glue.

TOOLS AND MATERIALS

METAL

FABRIC

PVA GLUE

SMALL BRUSH

CLOTH TO WIPE AWAY GLUE

MASKING TAPE

BANGLE
by Vannetta Seecharran
This slender bangle uses loops of folded ribbon to soften the hard edges of the silver setting.

Tip
Don't apply too much glue – some glue dries hard and is difficult to remove.

GLUING FABRIC TO METAL

1 APPLYING GLUE
This method also applies to gluing other materials to metal. Apply a small amount of glue to the metal with a brush; in this example, it has been applied inside the slot on the edge of the bangle.

2 APPLYING THE FABRIC
Insert the fabric into the slot. Some glue may squeeze onto the fabric, this can be wiped off with a cloth. Leave the glue to dry. The drying time will vary for different glues.

GLUING ENDS

1 PREPARE THE FABRIC
Cut a piece of masking tape to fit the end of the fabric and wrap it around once. This technique applies to pieces that have frayed edges and may not be suitable for cords or ribbons.

2 APPLYING GLUE
Use a small brush to apply some glue to the end of the fabric covered by the tape.

3 JOINING FABRIC AND METAL
Insert the end into the metal piece and leave it to dry. Don't attempt to handle it before it's completely dry.

MAKING CORDS

CORD IS MADE FROM SEVERAL STRANDS OF THREAD TWISTED TOGETHER, AND YOU CAN MAKE YOUR OWN ON WHICH TO HANG A PIECE OF JEWELLERY.

Cords are made of two or more threads twisted together and counter-twisted to increase the thickness. Cords can be made from fabric threads or plastic strips either by twisting with an electric drill or by hand. The material used needs to have some flexibility to allow the strands to twist. Cords made in this way can untwist easily, so the ends must be secured by sealing or gluing them. The strands you start with need to be four times the length of the final cord to allow for them being twisted tightly, then folded and counter-twisted.

Cord for hanging a pendant can be made from cotton or silk threads, and you can use several strands. The thickness of the finished cord depends on the number of strands that you use.

TOOLS AND MATERIALS

YARN OR THREAD

THICK METAL ROD

PENCIL OR AN ELECTRIC HAND DRILL WITH HOOK ATTACHMENT

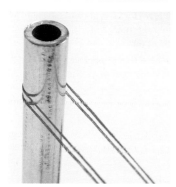

1 SECURING THE STRANDS
Cut two strands of yarn or thread to four times the length of the finished cord you want. Fix a metal rod in a vice. Wrap the strands in half around the rod. If you don't have a rod and vice, use a doorknob as a fixed point on which to secure the ends of threads when you are making cords.

2 TIE THE ENDS TOGETHER
Bring the ends of the thread together and make an overhand knot.

3 SPINNING
You can use either an electric hand drill with a hook on the end or a pencil for this step. Place the hook or pencil inside the knot. Turn on the drill to twist the strands or twist the pencil if you are doing it by hand. Twist until the strands are tight and feel springy.

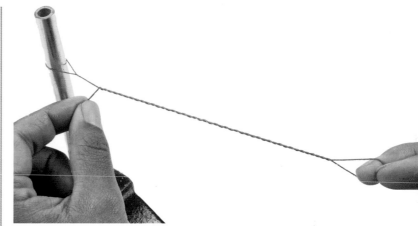

4 FOLDING IN HALF
Remove the hook and hold the strands firmly with one hand. Place the other hand in the middle of the twisted strands. Fold the strands in half and counter-twist them – you should naturally feel the direction to twist them. If you accidently let go, they will begin to twist themselves. You should now have a cord.

5 THE FINISHED CORD
Cut the knot to tidy the end. Pass the cord over steam to set it and keep it from untwisting. Secure the ends with a little glue; you can attach some kind of end clasp if you like, as shown here.

CROCHET

CROCHETING TECHNIQUES CAN
BE USED TO MAKE BEAUTIFUL
JEWELLERY AND CAN BE ADAPTED
IN MANY WAYS FROM
CROCHETING A CHAIN TO
ENCAPSULATING OBJECTS.

Crochet is a way of creating fabric from yarn or thread using a crochet hook. The fabric is created with a series of loops that join together to make a chain. A second row of chain can then be linked to the beginning of the first row and these chains build up to form a cloth. Round shapes can be created simply by increasing the number of loops in each row. Organic objects such as semi-precious stones can be crocheted around, for example, to create a casing for pendants.

A crochet hook is like a short knitting needle with a hook on one end. The hook can be made from metal, wood or plastic. Hooks come in a range of diameters, and the diameter determines the stitch size. Cotton, wool and ribbon threads are just a few of the materials that can be used for crocheting.

TOOLS AND MATERIALS

CROCHET HOOK

YARN

CHUNKY METAL CHAIN

CROCHET EARRINGS
by Karla Scharbert
These earrings were made
by crocheting around glass
beads with cotton thread.

MAKING A CHAIN

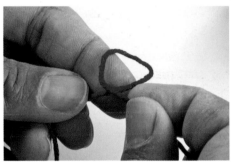

1 STARTING OFF
Take a length of yarn and hold the end in one hand. Make a loop with the short thread going under the longer length.

2 PULLING THROUGH
Hold the crochet hook in your other hand and place it inside loop. Pull the long end of yarn through the loop.

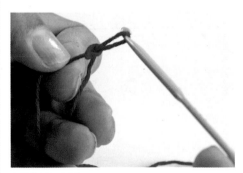

3 FIRST LOOP
Hold the short end of the yarn with your thumb and index finger and the long end with the your other fingers. Pull the loop to make a knot.

EMBELLISHED BRACELET
by Brian Whitewick

This bracelet takes the principle of crocheting around a metal chain and pushes it further, by using two different colours of yarn and different crochet stitches.

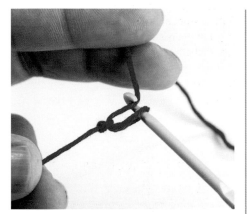

4 MAKING THE FIRST LINK
Keep the hook inside the loop. Grab the long yarn with the hook and pull it through the loop.

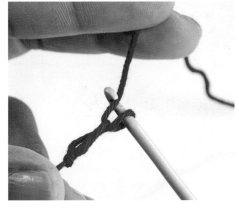

6 MAKING THE SECOND LINK
Pull the yarn tight to increase the tension, grab the long yarn with the hook, and pull it through the loop.

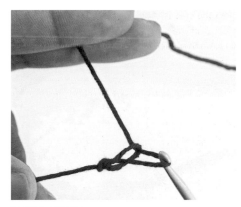

5 PULL TIGHT
Pull the yarn to make the knot tight. Keep the hook inside the loop. Pull the long yarn to reduce the loop around the needle.

7 MAKING A CHAIN
Repeat Step 6 to make another link and repeat this process until you have made the desired length of chain. A very long length can be used to make a necklace by wrapping it around the neck several times.

CROCHET NECKLACE
by Joanne Haywood

This necklace was constructed from multiple oxidized silver chains and crocheted balls in red and dark grey.

CROCHETING AROUND AN OBJECT

Once you've mastered the basic crochet technique, you can crochet around objects, such as the chunky metal chain shown here.

2 MAKING THE FIRST LINK

You now have your first stitch. Next, pull the yarn tight through the chain link and over the hook, taking care not to release the yarn from the hook. Keep some tension in the long yarn end by holding it with your other hand.

3 MAKING THE SECOND STITCH

This time, working from the outside of the link, grab the long yarn with the hook and pull it through the loop on the hook. This forms the second stitch.

1 STARTING OFF

Follow Steps 1, 2 and 3 from Making a chain, to make a loop. Hold the short end of the yarn between your thumb and index finger just below the loop. Place the loop on top of the chain link and the long end of the yarn underneath. Insert the hook through the chain link, grab the long yarn end, and pull it back through the link.

THE FINISHED PIECE

The finished chain has a bright red crochet embellishment, which could be applied to many other items in the same way. As shown here, you could add further rows of crochet to the piece.

4 MAKING THE THIRD STITCH

Pass the long end of the yarn back to the inside of the chain link, insert the hook into the centre of the chain link, and pull it through the loop on your hook. This is the third stitch. For the fourth stitch, working again from the outside of the chain link, pull the fourth stitch through the loop on the hook. This is a chain, just as described in the Making a chain sequence, with the difference that it is formed around another object. Repeat these steps, passing the yarn over and under the link until you have stitched the length you need.

PLEATING AND SHAPING

PLEATING IS THE PROCESS OF MAKING CREASES IN A SHEET OF FABRIC. THE FABRIC IS FOLDED AND STEAMED OR PRESSED TO MAKE THE FOLDS PERMANENT. FABRIC CAN ALSO BE SHAPED BY STEAMING IT WRAPPED AROUND OBJECTS.

Pleating can be done with any fabric and is made permanent by sewing, pressing or heat steaming. It is a well-known technique that is used for making clothing and upholstery and can also be applied to jewellery making. There are many types of pleats and most are a variation on a few basic kinds. Accordion pleats, demonstrated here, are basic pleats consisting of a series of folds of equal width stacked on top of each other and, if ironed flat, they become knife pleats. Knife pleats are common in dressmaking and are sometimes sewn halfway, allowing for movement in the other half. Pleats can be made in any size and used in any part of a design.

Heat steaming is a process for manipulating or sculpting a piece of fabric into a permanent shape. Small objects such as beads can be used to create dome shapes in fabric, and pleats can be made by folding a piece of fabric in paper. After steaming, shapes are permanently fixed in the fabric and cannot be removed. The pleated fabric can be washed, sewn and cut after it has been steamed. This technique is suitable for synthetic fabrics.

Pleating is not an obvious technique to use for jewellery making; however, fabric can be pleated and sewn together to make necklaces and bracelets.

TOOLS AND MATERIALS

PAPER

FINE SYNTHETIC FABRIC

STRING OR RUBBER BAND

LARGE HEATPROOF PAN

COLANDER

HEATPROOF GLOVES

SMALL OBJECTS TO TIE IN FABRIC

NEEDLE OR DRESSMAKING PINS

STEAM PLEATING

2 FOLDING THE PAPER
Hold the ends of the paper and fold them over. Run your finger along the fold to crease it.

1 PREPARING THE FABRIC
This technique works best with fine synthetic fabric such as polyester, and it can be cut to any size or shape. Cut a piece of paper about 2.5cm (1in) larger than the fabric. Place the fabric on top of the paper.

Tip
Use dress pins to secure pleats if you are ironing them to make them permanent.

3 MAKING A SECOND FOLD

Hold both ends of the first fold and put one finger under the first fold and one on top. Fold the paper under the first pleat and crease. Make another fold the same width as the first and repeat this step until you have folded the entire fabric and it looks like a stack of folds.

4 CREASING THE STACK

Run your fingers along the stack of folds to crease it well.

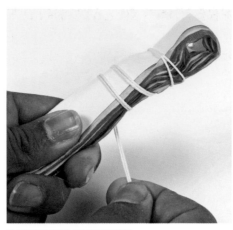

5 SECURING THE STACK

You can fold the stack in half, into quarters, or any other shape. Tie it securely with a piece of string or a rubber band.

THE PLEATED FABRIC

The pleated fabric can be cut and sewn at this stage to make a piece of jewellery.

6 STEAMING

Fill a large heatproof pan with 5cm (2in) water and place a metal colander or sieve over the pan. The colander should not touch the water. Bring the water to the boil until it is producing steam. Wearing heatproof gloves, place the fabric inside the colander and leave it to steam gently for an hour. Cover the pan for a quicker steaming time and monitor the level of liquid so that it doesn't dry out. You can steam more than one piece of fabric at a time; here, two pieces are steamed simultaneously.

7 DRYING

Wearing a pair of heatproof gloves, remove the fabric from the pan – take care when opening the pan, do not position your face over it. Leave the fabric to dry before carefully unfolding it and removing the paper. If the fabric has not set in the desired shape, place it back in the steamer for a further thirty minutes, or until it has a permanent shape.

SHAPING FABRIC

PRESSING PLEATS INTO FABRIC

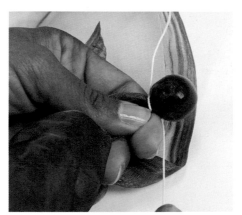

1 TIE SMALL OBJECTS IN THE FABRIC

Lay your fabric on a flat surface and place small objects, such as beads, underneath. Wrap the objects inside the fabric and tie them in place with a piece of string or a rubber band. You can wrap several objects in one piece of fabric. Steam the fabric as before.

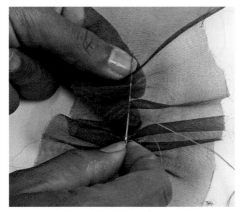

1 MAKING WRINKLED PLEATS

Make irregular folds in the fine synthetic fabric you have chosen and secure them with a needle or dressmaking pins. Here, a threaded needle was used. The fabric could also be pinned onto a soft surface and ironed over.

THE FINISHED PLEATS

Once pressed, the irregular folds are permanently set in the fabric.

2 THE FINISHED SHAPED FABRIC

The fabric has been steamed and some of the beads removed, leaving a series of beautiful rounded shapes.

2 PRESSING

Using a domestic iron, set the temperature to medium. Place the folded fabric on an ironing board and iron until the folds are set in the fabric. Test the iron on a scrap of fabric first to find the ideal heat – remember that a hot iron will melt synthetic fabrics.

SLEEVE

by Vannetta Seecharran

This decorative fabric sleeve is folded and pleated.

FLOCKING

FLOCKING IS A PROCESS USED TO PRODUCE A FABRIC-LIKE COATING TO COVER ALMOST ANY SURFACE. THE FLOCK TEXTURE IS SOFT AND SMOOTH, WHICH MAKES IT VERY SUITABLE FOR JEWELLERY MAKING. AN EXTENSIVE RANGE OF COLOURS AND TEXTURES IS AVAILABLE.

TOOLS AND MATERIALS

MASKING TAPE

ITEM TO BE FLOCKED

FLOCKING FIBRE

HANDHELD FLOCKING UNIT

ADHESIVE

SCREEN

SQUEEGEE

DUST MASK

BROOCH
by Zoe Robertson
This flocked brooch is set into a bezel mount like a cabochon might be set into a ring.

Flocking can be achieved by a number of different methods, but electrostatic flocking is probably the method most accessible to the jeweller. The process applies special fibres, called 'flock', onto a surface that has been coated with an adhesive. Flock is the term for specially cut lengths of nylon or rayon fibres, which are available in various lengths from 0.5mm (1⁄64in) to 3mm (1⁄8in) and in a very wide range of colours. Several finishes are possible, such as suede or velvet. Almost any surface can be flocked, including fabric, leather and paper, as long as you use an adhesive suitable for the material. The adhesive can be sprayed on or applied with a screen. The electrostatic flocking process uses a handheld unit that applies an electrostatic charge to the flock so that the fibres are drawn towards a grounded metal plate and penetrate 'end on' into the adhesive to produce a seamless, fabric-like surface.

The flocking fibres adhere to the surface, but they can be scraped off, so flocking should only be applied to finished pieces. If flocking fibres adhere to any unwanted areas, they can be removed with fine-grade sandpaper. Areas of a finished piece can be masked with tape to stop the flock from adhering to them. For example, the edge of a piece can be masked so that there is a clean edge once the piece is flocked, or a striped design can be created by masking parts of a piece and flocking the unmasked areas. Always wear a dust mask and work in a well-ventilated area when flocking.

FLOCKING TECHNIQUE

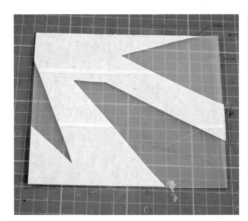

1 MASKING AREAS
Place tape on the areas where you do not want the flock to adhere, if masking is part of your design.

2 APPLYING ADHESIVE
Apply an even amount of adhesive to the surface to be flocked. You can either spray the adhesive or apply it using a screen (as shown here) to achieve an even application. Place the screen over the piece to be flocked and apply adhesive to one end of the screen.

3 SPREADING THE ADHESIVE

Place the squeegee in front of the adhesive and pull it across the screen. When you lift the screen your piece should be covered with adhesive.

4 ATTACHING THE PIECE TO THE FLOCKING PLATE

Clip the piece to the metal flocking plate. Place it in front of the plate.

5 DUSTING THE PIECE WITH FLOCK

Fill the flocking machine with flock. Hold the plate at a slight angle and dust the flock onto the piece. Try to apply a thin, even layer across the entire piece. Remember to work in a well-ventilated area and wear a dust mask.

6 DUSTING OFF

Tap the piece lightly to remove any loose flock.

7 REMOVING THE TAPE

Carefully remove the tape from one corner of the piece. Don't try to pull all the tape off at the same time.

THE FINISHED PIECE

The flock will adhere to the surface where adhesive was applied. You can simply blow off any loose fibres.

Tips

• *Take care not to inhale the flocking fibres. Wear a dust mask.*
• *Flocking fibres are very small and flocking needs to be done in a well-ventilated area.*

Flocking fibres

CHAPTER 4

PAPER
AND PAPER
PULP

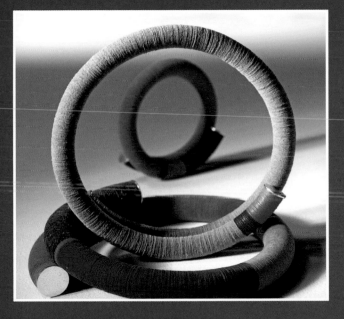

This step-by-step guide will take you through the techniques of folding, cutting and printing on paper, and how to apply them to jewellery making. It will also demonstrate how making paper is an excellent way to create materials to use in your jewellery designs.

NECKLACE *(opposite)*
by Naoko Yoshizawa
Necklace contructed using handmade Japanese paper and thread.

NECKPIECES AND BANGLES
(centre left)
by Angela O'Kelly
These pieces were made using fabric, paper, plastic, steel wire and silver.

BROOCHES *(centre right)*
by Naoko Yoshizawa
Handmade Japanese paper, oxidized silver and gold-plated bronze.

SCULPTURAL ARMPIECES
(top right)
by Angela O'Kelly
Armpieces made using fabric, paper, plastic, felt and elastic.

PAPER AND PAPER PULP PROPERTIES

PAPER CAN BE USED TO MAKE PIECES OF JEWELLERY, AND IT HAS A NUMBER OF USEFUL PROPERTIES, SUCH AS LOW COST, THE EASE WITH WHICH IT CAN BE CUT AND SHAPED, AND THE FACT THAT IT CAN BE PRINTED ON. THERE ARE SOME DIFFICULTIES THOUGH, WHICH NEED TO BE OVERCOME, SUCH AS ITS RELATIVE WEAKNESS AND ITS LACK OF DURABILITY.

Paper is used widely by contemporary jewellers, in a variety of ways, ranging from cast objects to constructed three-dimensional forms. It is available in sheets in varying thicknesses. You can make new sheets of paper from recycled paper and incorporate small objects, such as leaves, confetti or gold leaf, by mixing them with the pulp before casting to create decorative effects. Damp sheets can also be pressed into or over a mould to create permanent three-dimensional shapes.

Jewellery made from paper lacks a certain amount of permanence and can

METALLIC AND IRIDESCENT PAPER

PLAIN PAPER

PATTERNED PAPER

be destroyed easily – one possibility for overcoming this is to laminate a sheet of synthetic paper to make it waterproof. In some cases, the conceptual idea behind the piece is for it to lack permanence and to use the fragility of the paper to an advantage. Paper can be glued with contact-cement glue used for leather or white paper glue, which is available from craft suppliers.

DESIGNING WITH PAPER AND PAPER PULP

Qualities Strong but fragile, recycled, structured, flexible, transparent or opaque.

Applications Damp paper or paper pulp can be moulded into three-dimensional shapes. Structured shapes can be created by cutting and folding. Thin sheets of paper can be laminated together to increase thickness or to be carved. Paper can also be recycled and made into new sheets with gold leaf and flower petals added to the pulp. Paper can be twisted, rolled and folded, and patterns can be printed on its surface.

Combining with other materials Paper is most commonly combined with metal; however, it can be combined with most other materials as well. Methods of attaching paper to other materials include gluing, riveting and stitching.

Where to look for inspiration Take a look at the websites below for inspiration from jewellers working with paper and paper pulp.
• **Jo Pond, United Kingdom**
www.jopond.com
Paper, found objects and silver are used to create beautiful narrative jewellery.
• **Angela O Kelly, United Kingdom**
www.angelaokelly.com
Paper and mixed-media jewellery, exploring colour.
• **Nel Linssen, Netherlands**
www.nellinssen.nl
Paper jewellery, predominantly neckpieces and bracelets.

HANDMADE PAPER, ROSE PETALS AND GOLD LEAF

ADHESIVE TAPES INCLUDING MASKING TAPE

SCREEN PRINTING

SCREEN PRINTING IS A USEFUL METHOD OF PRINTING A DESIGN ONTO THE SURFACE OF A MATERIAL THAT IS GOING TO FORM PART OF A PIECE OF JEWELLERY. IT IS PARTICULARLY APPROPRIATE WHEN YOU ARE MAKING JEWELLERY WITH A PLASTIC SHEET (SEE PAGE 60).

Screen printing uses a screen and a stencil to evenly distribute ink onto a surface in a particular pattern. The screen is a fine woven mesh stretched over a frame and is usually made from steel, nylon or polyester. The stencil is a negative of the pattern to be printed, so the ink only passes through the mesh where the stencil is open. A stencil can be made by cutting a pattern out of a non-permeable material such as paper and can then be attached to the screen, as shown here. More

TOOLS AND MATERIALS

SCREEN

MESH

MASKING TAPE

SCRAP PAPER

PAPER STENCIL

INKS

BINDER

PAPER

SPOON

SQUEEGEE

SPONGE

BASIC TECHNIQUE

1 PREPARING THE SCREEN
Place the screen with the mesh side up. Check the back of the screen for unexposed areas. Ink can leak out of the corners, so to stop this happening, apply masking tape to the corners.

2 MAKING A TEMPLATE FOR PRINTING
In this example, a blank screen is used with a paper stencil that has been cut from a sheet of paper.

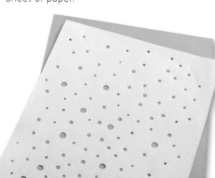

3 PREPARATION
Lay scrap paper on your work surface before you start, to protect the surface. Place the printing material on top of the scrap paper. Place the stencil on the printing paper and the screen on top.

complicated stencilling can be achieved using a technique called photo emulsion.

The method shown here applies to all screen-printing processes, though the inks and mesh sizes used will depend on the printing material. Fabrics require a coarser mesh than plastics. It is important that the mesh size is appropriate for the ink or the screen can become blocked. Check with your ink supplier to get the correct size mesh for the ink you are using.

Screen printing for jewellery should be done on the raw material before it is made into jewellery and, if printing is integral to the design, you will need to plan carefully where the printed areas of the design will be.

Acrylic-based inks are used for printing on paper, and they need an appropriate binder. The proportion of ink to binder is about half and half; the more binder there is in relation to ink, the more transparent the ink will be.

4 MIXING THE INK
Mix the binder with the ink. Remember that more binder will make the ink more transparent. Stir well until all the ink is mixed with the binder.

6 USING THE SQUEEGEE
If possible, ask someone to help you hold the screen. Place the squeegee behind the ink and pull the ink towards you to the other side of the screen. Tap the squeegee lightly on the mesh and push the ink back to the other side, where you started from. Make some test prints to check that the image is printing and to determine how many pulls are necessary.

7 REMOVING THE SCREEN
Carefully lift the screen to reveal the print. The paper stencil may still be attached to the back of the screen and can be removed or used to make another print.

5 APPLYING THE INK
Apply an even amount of ink along the top edge of the screen, using a spoon to distribute it.

Tip
Before you make the final print, do some test prints to determine the quality of the print and the number of pulls required.

8 WASHING THE SCREEN
Hold the screen under running water and scrub the ink off with a sponge. Clean both sides of the screen to ensure that all the ink has been removed. Allow the screen to dry completely before using it again.

CUTTING AND LAMINATING

YOU CAN LAMINATE SHEETS OF PAPER TOGETHER TO INCREASE THE THICKNESS. THIS TECHNIQUE MAKES THE PAPER MORE DURABLE FOR JEWELLERY MAKING; YOU CAN THEN CUT IT WITH A LASER CUTTER OR SHARP CRAFT KNIFE.

Cutting paper with a craft knife is straightforward. A template made from metal or another firm material can be used to guide the blade around curved shapes. To guarantee a smooth line, it's important to use a sharp knife.

Laminating sheets of paper together increases the paper thickness and may be necessary if a paper needs additional support. In jewellery making, paper can easily get damaged and, to improve its usability, it can be laminated with other materials, such as linen or synthetic paper. The glue you use needs to be strong enough to hold the sheets together without buckling. Buckling is usually a problem when laminating large sheets – to avoid this problem, rub over the paper with a soft cloth to smooth it. In the example shown here, a contact cement is used, which is a strong bonding glue used for paper, wood or leather. Follow the application instructions for the glue you are using.

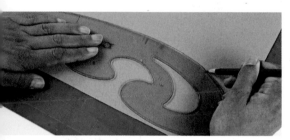

1 DRAWING THE DESIGN
Draw your design on the back of the paper. If your design includes curved shapes, you may find it easier to make a template and trace around it.

2 CUTTING OUT THE DESIGN
You can cut thin sheets of paper with a pair of sharp scissors, or use a sharp craft knife to cut the paper to the desired shape. Use a ruler or a template to help you with straight and curved edges.

TOOLS AND MATERIALS
SHEET OF PAPER
PEN OR PENCIL
TEMPLATE (OPTIONAL)
SCISSORS
SHARP CRAFT KNIFE AND CUTTING MAT
RULER (OPTIONAL)
CONTACT-CEMENT GLUE

3 GLUING THE SHEETS
Apply a thin layer of glue to the back of both pieces of paper and leave them to dry.

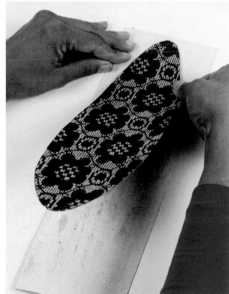

4 PUTTING THE SHEETS TOGETHER
Lay one piece of paper with the glue side facing up and hold the other piece with the glue side facing down. Press them together and smooth them with your hands or a soft cloth.

FOLDING AND PLEATING

PAPER CAN BE FOLDED AND PLEATED BY SCORING WITH A KNIFE IN SPECIFIED AREAS. THIS FOLDED PAPER CAN BE USED TO MAKE PIECES OF JEWELLERY OR FOR PROTOTYPING WORK IN OTHER MATERIALS (THE STAGE BEFORE A FINAL PIECE IS MADE).

Paper is reasonably easy to work with and can be cut and scored with a sharp knife. The back of the knife can be used to make a dent in the paper so that it can be folded into shape. Thicker cards may need to be scored halfway through the thickness to get a sharp line before folding and can be reinforced with tape on the underside to keep them from tearing.

Paper is a great material with which to make a prototype. Prototyping is ideal for developing a design and for experimenting with ideas. You will find that paper can be folded and manipulated in a variety of ways to make three-dimensional shapes.

<table>
<tr><td>TOOLS AND MATERIALS</td></tr>
<tr><td>PAPER</td></tr>
<tr><td>CUTTING MAT</td></tr>
<tr><td>PENCIL</td></tr>
<tr><td>KNIFE</td></tr>
</table>

PAPER-WORKING TECHNIQUES

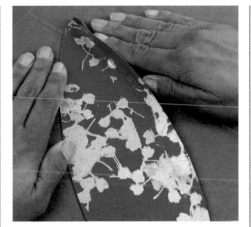

2 FOLDING
Turn the paper over so that the scored line is underneath. Fold the paper over along the scored line from one end to the other. Rub your fingers along the fold to make it permanent.

3 FORMING THE FINISHED SHAPE
In this example, the paper is made into a bracelet, and the ends can be connected with a clasp or a cufflink via a hole in both ends.

1 SCORING
Place the paper on a cutting mat with the back facing up. Use a pencil to draw a light line on the paper where it will be folded. Use the back of a cutting knife and go over the pencil line. In this example, two sheets have been glued together (see page 108), but this technique can also be done with a single sheet of paper.

Tips
• *Glue and tape can be used to secure edges when you are making three-dimensional shapes.*
• *When folding thick paper, do it slowly to ensure that the paper creases in the right place.*

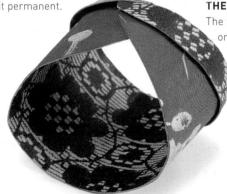

THE FINISHED PIECE
The finished bracelet not only looks effective, with its double-sided paper patterns, but also the process of laminating has strengthened it.

▶

CUTTING AND SHAPING

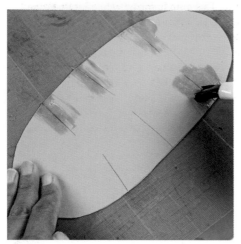

1 MAKING CUTS
To create a simple three-dimensional shape, take a piece of stiff paper and make a series of cuts along the top and bottom of the shape. Apply a thin layer of glue over the cuts. This technique can be done with any shape of paper.

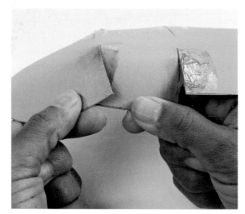

2 PLEATING
Hold the paper in your hand and overlap the edges of the cuts. The paper will begin to take on a three-dimensional form.

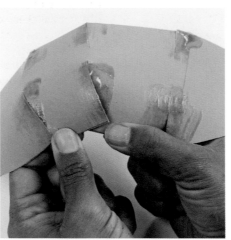

3 REPEAT THE PROCESS
Turn the shape around and repeat the pleating process on the other edge.

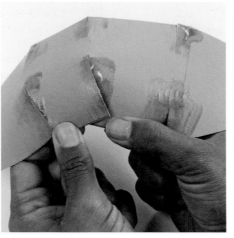

4 THE FINISHED SHAPE
This kind of technique is useful for prototyping metal forms. You could use any shape or thickness of paper.

FOLDED METAL NECKLACE
by Melanie Eddy
A folding technique was used to create this necklace. Several prototypes were made in paper, and the design was then transferred to metal.

PAPERMAKING

PAPER IS A POPULAR MATERIAL, OFTEN USED BY CONTEMPORARY JEWELLERS. IT CAN BE USED IN A VARIETY OF WAYS FROM CUTTING OUT TO BEING PRINTED ON OR EVEN SCULPTED.

A new sheet of paper can be made from old recycled paper. The paper is cut into small pieces, soaked for a few hours until it is soft, and then blended to a pulp. This pulp is mixed with a large amount of water and then spread out on a screen to strain out the liquid. The sheet of pulp is turned out onto a cloth and left to dry. Confetti or small flowers can be added at two points: either in the pulp mixture or when the pulp is lifted from the screen before turning out.

Diluted paper glue can be added to the pulp mixture for extra strength, but this is not essential. The finished colour of the paper will be the same colour as the starting paper and the final sheet will be about a quarter of the size of the paper use to make the pulp.

MAKING PAPER

1 PREPARATIONS
Select two trays: one that the screen can move around in freely and the other to soak the paper. Also, prepare the surface on which to turn out the paper by spreading a sheet of plastic on the surface near the tray and laying two pieces of kitchen paper on top. Cut the paper into 6-mm (¼-in) squares. The smaller the pieces the easier it will be to make pulp.

TOOLS AND MATERIALS

TWO TRAYS

SCREEN

SHEET OF PLASTIC

KITCHEN PAPER

PAPER TO RECYCLE

BLENDER

CLOTHS

SPONGE

HEAVY BOARD

2 SOAKING THE PAPER
Soak the paper for a few hours, until it is soft. The thicker the paper, the longer it will need to be soaked.

3 BLENDING
Fill half the blender with water and add some soaked paper. The proportion is 1 part paper to 3 parts water. Blend the paper until it is a fine pulp.

4 ADDING THE PULP
Fill the tray with enough water to cover the bottom, blend the pulp in batches, and add it to the tray. The amount of pulp in the water will determine the thickness of the paper. At this stage you can add small objects such as confetti or small flowers.

5 SUBMERGING THE SCREEN
Stir the pulp and hold the screen with the mesh facing up. Slip one end into the pulp until the entire screen is submerged in the mixture.

▶

6 LIFTING THE SCREEN
Grip the screen on either side and lift it out of
the pulp mixture, at the same time as shaking
it gently back and forth to drain the water and
settle the fibres. At this stage you can add
small objects such as confetti or small flowers.

8 SPONGING
The back of the screen should be facing up.
Carefully press a sponge around the mesh to
absorb as much excess water as possible and
to bind the paper fibres together.

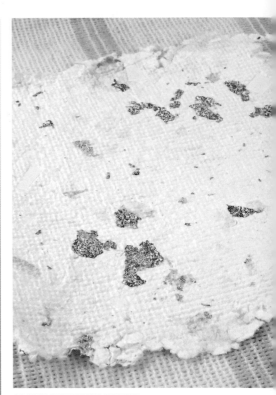

10 THE FINISHED PAPER
The finished, dried paper can be handled
and used to make jewellery pieces.

7 TURNING OUT THE PULP
Flip the screen onto the cloth so the pulp
is facing down.

9 LIFTING THE SCREEN
Carefully lift the screen to release the paper.
Allow the paper to dry completely before
handling it. For a flat sheet, place another
cloth over the wet paper and lay a heavy
board on top.

Tip
*You could make your own screen by
stretching a pair of old stockings across a
wire frame, or some kind of mesh stretched
over an old picture frame would work. It is
essential that the screen is tight and fine
enough to allow the water to drain through
but not the pulp.*

PAPER CASTING

A SHEET OF PAPER CAN BE SCULPTED INTO A THREE-DIMENSIONAL SHAPE BY PRESSING INTO OR OVER A MOULD.

Wet sheets of paper can be pressed into or around a mould and will remain in the shape of the mould when dried. Sheets can be soaked or made from paper pulp for jewellery making. You can make shapes such as domes and use them alone or in combination with metal for pieces of jewellery. Moulds can be made from plaster, rubber or brass (steel will rust if wet). You will need to use a release agent with plaster moulds to prevent the paper from sticking.

Paper pulp can be used before it is made into sheets of paper, but it does need to be fairly thick so that small amounts can be lifted and packed into the mould. Diluted paper glue can be added to a pulp mixture before casting, for additional strength.

MOULDING A SIMPLE PAPER SHAPE

TOOLS AND MATERIALS

PAPER OR PAPER PULP

MOULD

SCISSORS

1 STARTING SHEET
Use the pulp from papermaking (see page 111) or soak a new sheet of paper until it is soft. Cut a piece of paper slightly bigger than the mould.

2 PRESSING INTO THE MOULD
If you are using sheet paper, place it over the mould and gently press into the mould. If you are using pulp, take a small amount in your hand and press it flat before pressing it into the mould. In this example, a doming block and punch are being used. If it is a big mould, use your fingers to press the paper in. Additional layers can be added to increase the thickness. Leave the paper to dry completely. You don't have to stick to domes; any shape can be used as a mould for paper.

Tip
If the paper tears while you are pressing it into the mould, it can be repaired with another piece of paper over the top. Don't be tempted to remove it from the mould while it is wet.

3 REMOVING THE SHAPE FROM THE MOULD
As the paper dries it will shrink and pull away from the mould and can be lifted out easily.

4 FINISHED MOULDED PIECES
Excess paper can be trimmed from the shapes, and they are now ready to use.

THE FINISHED JEWELLERY
In this example, the paper dome has been used to make an earring.

MASKING TAPE

MASKING TAPE CAN BE CUT, STITCHED AND SCREEN PRINTED. IT IS AN EASY MATERIAL TO USE TO CREATE INTERESTING JEWELLERY PIECES.

Masking tape can be made into sheets by sticking the edges of several lengths together. Cut lengths with a pair of scissors or a craft knife to make smaller pieces that are more useful for jewellery. Fabric buttons can be covered and sewn onto a sheet and strips of paper can be sandwiched between the sheets to give the tape structure.

As the tape ages it will become discoloured and fragile, so do bear this in mind when you are designing. Tape is available in several strengths, rated on a 1–100 scale, based on the strength of the adhesive.

TOOLS AND MATERIALS

MASKING TAPE

CUTTING MAT

KNIFE

PAPER

METAL RULER

SCISSORS

CIRCULAR COVERABLE BUTTONS

CIRCLE TEMPLATE

MAKING A BUTTON NECKLACE

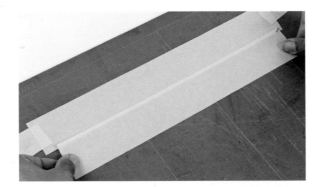

1 STARTING A SHEET
Cut a length of tape and lay it on a cutting mat with the sticky side facing up. Use some smaller pieces to secure it to the mat. Cut another piece the same length as the first and lay it on the first strip, overlapping the edges. Repeat the process until you have the desired width. You can use a combination of different widths to make one sheet.

2 SANDWICHING STRIPS OF PAPER
Lay thin strips of paper on the sheet of tape. The spacing can be random or regular to suit your design. This step is not essential, but the paper will give the sheet more structure.

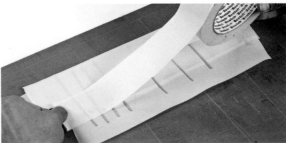

3 COMPLETING THE SHEET
Lay a strip of masking tape over the sheet, overlapping the edges.

CHOKER
by Vannetta Seecharran
Buttons were covered in paper and stitched to fabric for this piece.

4 CUTTING THE SHEET
You can cut the sheet into any shape using a sharp knife and a metal ruler or a pair of scissors. The finished sheet can be cut, sewn and used to make jewellery pieces.

5 COVERING BUTTONS
Choose the type of button you would like to cover. Use a circle template to find the correct size to cover the button.

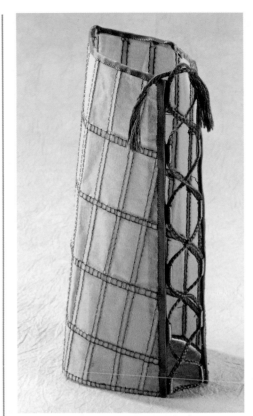

ARMLET
by Vannetta Seecharran
Several sheets of masking tape were taped together with strips of paper between them. The paper strips were stitched over by hand. Since the piece was made, the tape has aged and become transparent.

6 DRAWING A CIRCLE
Fix a piece of tape onto the cutting mat and draw the correct size circle on the tape.

7 CUTTING OUT
Peel the tape off the cutting mat and cut around the circle.

10 USING THE COVERED BUTTONS
You could make many covered buttons and stitch them onto a strip of masking tape, as shown here.

THE FINISHED PIECE
The finished necklace is joined with a button clasp.

8 FOLDING OVER THE EDGES
Turn the button over so the bottom is facing up and stick it in the centre of the tape circle. Fold the edges over towards the inside of the button.

9 PUTTING ON THE BACK
Place the button back inside the button and press until it snaps securely into place.

CHAPTER 5

OTHER MATERIALS

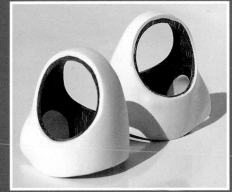

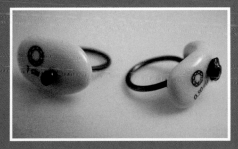

CLUSTER RINGS *(opposite)*
by Frieda Munro
Silver rings, each sandwiched between
two layers of Formica.

RINGS *(centre left)*
by Ruth Tomlinson
Precious metal rings with delicate
porcelain flowers for decoration.

UNICATED RINGS *(top right)*
by Kisten Bak
Rings made from a core of wood
covered in a layer of resin.

RINGS *(bottom right)*
by Daisy Choi
Crackle-glazed porcelain is
mounted onto a silver ring shank
for these pieces.

The materials included in this chapter are not traditionally
associated with jewellery making, but they can be very
successfully applied to the craft. Casting with concrete and
fusing glass sheets can create effective and unusual pieces
of jewellery, and handmade ceramic beads can add colour
and interest to beaded jewellery.

OTHER MATERIALS AND THEIR PROPERTIES

THE MATERIALS FEATURED IN THIS CHAPTER ARE 'BORROWED' FROM OTHER CRAFT AREAS, AND EACH IS REALLY A WHOLE SUBJECT IN ITSELF. IN THIS CHAPTER, THE TECHNIQUES ARE SIMPLIFIED TO DEMONSTRATE HOW THEY CAN BE ADAPTED TO JEWELLERY MAKING.

CLAY: Clay can be manipulated into any form to make jewellery beads or hollow shapes such as pottery and tableware. The soft, malleable nature of clay makes it an easy material to work with as a beginner, and you can choose from a variety of clays. Some clay does not require firing and can be decorated and allowed to air dry, but the majority of clays need to be fired at a high temperature (bisque fired), and at this point, decorative patterns can be painted on as glaze and fired again to set them.

GLASS SHEET, RODS AND CONFETTI

CHERRY AND WALNUT WOOD

CLAY

WOOD: Wood is a versatile material that lends itself to jewellery making, and there are many types to choose from. Wood can be carved, sculpted or inlaid with metal pieces, and a variety of surface finishes can be applied, such as paint, varnish or wax.

CONCRETE: Concrete is a material composed of cement, water and sand, which are mixed together to form a mixture that can be poured into cavities. For jewellery making and casting small objects, a smooth mixture is necessary and very fine sand and cement should be used. Various aggregates such as coloured sand and metal filings can be added to cement to improve strength and appearance.

GLASS: Sheets of glass can be fused together in a kiln to make shapes ideal for pendants and earrings. Wires can be sandwiched between the sheets and glass 'confetti', small pieces of glass or powder, can be fused onto the surface for interesting effects. Fusing glass sheets is an easy and effective way of making interesting jewellery pieces.

SAND AND CEMENT

DESIGNING WITH OTHER MATERIALS

Qualities
- Wood: sturdy, textured, grainy.
- Concrete: industrial, rough.
- Glass: smooth, transparent, fragile, colourful.
- Ceramic: soft, malleable, durable.

Applications
- Wood can be easily carved and shaped and is ideal for making jewellery. The surface can be varnished to enhance the texture and natural colour or it can be coloured with enamel paint.
- Concrete can be set into metal shapes or into a mould to make pieces of jewellery. Its industrial look contrasts well with precious metals such as silver and gold.
- Glass sheets can be fused together to create colourful pendants and earrings. 'Confetti' can be fused to the surface for decoration.
- Clay can be sculpted into beads and other shapes to make jewellery. The surface can be painted with colourful glazes and fired.

Combining with other materials Concrete and wood can be combined with metal and plastic, but it is difficult to combine glass and ceramic with other materials, other than as pendants or beads.

Where to look for inspiration Take a look at the websites below for inspiration from jewellers working with other materials.
- **Iris Bodemer, Germany**
www.irisbodemer.de
Innovative mixed-media works using a variety of textiles and found objects.
- **Alessia Semeraro, Italy**
www.alessiasemeraro.com
Wood and mixed-media jewellery.
- **Jacqueline Cullen, United Kingdom**
www.jacquelinecullen.com
Contemporary jet jewellery.

WOOD

ANY HARDWOOD CAN BE USED FOR MAKING JEWELLERY, AND VERY DENSE WOODS SUCH AS ROSEWOOD AND WALNUT ARE ESPECIALLY APPROPRIATE.

You can cut wood with a jewellery saw, a coping saw, an electric bandsaw or a laser-cutter. The required shape can be made roughly with a saw and then refined using a bench-mounted belt sander and finished by hand sanding. Automated laser-cutters, although expensive, can cut wood into very detailed shapes. A very effective way to use this in jewellery making is to create a series of thin sheets of wood in varying shapes and then laminate them together to make a three-dimensional shape.

Other materials such as silver, plastic or a different coloured wood can be inlaid into a wooden piece. You can do this relatively easily by using silver or plastic rods inserted into holes drilled in the wood. Other shapes such as strips can also be inlaid using the same method.

TOOLS AND MATERIALS

WOOD

PEN OR PENCIL

JEWELLERY SAW OR COPING SAW

BENCH-MOUNTED BELT SANDER OR COARSE FILES

COARSE SANDPAPER

FINE SANDPAPER

FINISHING WAX OR AGENT

SILVER WIRE OR OTHER PIECES TO BE INLAID

DRILL AND DRILL BIT

FLAT-NOSE PLIERS

GLUE

METAL BLOCK OR OTHER FIRM SURFACE

RIVETING HAMMER

FLAT FILE

METAL BURRS OR SHARP KNIFE

CREATING AN INLAID WOODEN PIECE

1 DRAWING THE DESIGN
Draw a design on the wood using a pen or pencil. You may find it easier to cut out the design from paper and trace around it onto the wood.

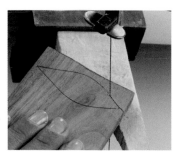

2 CUTTING OUT THE DESIGN
Use a jewellery saw or a coping saw to cut around the line.

3 SHAPING AND SANDING
Shape the wood either by sanding with a bench-mounted belt sander or using coarse files. Use coarse sandpaper suitable for wood to shape it further and smooth the surface. Next, use fine-grade sandpaper and rub until the surface feels smooth and all the scratches have been removed. At this stage you can apply a finishing wax or another finishing agent to seal the surface.

4 INLAYING ROUND PIECES
In this example, a piece of silver wire is being inlaid; however, other materials can be inlaid by the same method. Select a drill bit that is the same diameter as the piece to be inlaid. Drill a hole to half the depth of the wood. Cut the wire 1mm (1/32in) longer than the depth of the hole. Use a pair of flat-nose pliers to hold the wire and insert it into the hole. You can apply a small amount of glue to the wire before inserting it into the hole.

INLAYING A METAL STRIP

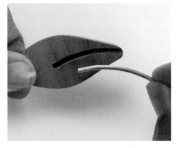

5 RIVETING
Place the piece on a metal block or a firm surface and use a riveting hammer to carefully tap the wire in the hole. Take care at this stage, as the wood can split if it is hammered too hard.

1 INLAYING A LONG PIECE
Carve a slot the same length and width as the piece to be inlaid. You can use metal burrs or a sharp knife to cut the slot.

6 FILING FLUSH
Hold the piece in your hand or rest it on a surface and file the top of the wire with a flat file to make it flush with the wood.

The stages of creating a solid wooden piece.

2 HAMMERING THE PIECE IN
Rest the wood on a metal block or firm surface and tap the metal into the slot with the riveting hammer. Apply a small amount of glue to the metal before tapping it in.

BANGLE IN WOOD AND SILVER
by Mette Jensen
This sculptural bangle was shaped with steam and the ends hidden and joined with a piece of silver.

WOOD INLAID WITH A SILVER STRIP
The finished pendant has been coated with finishing wax.

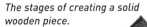

WOOD INLAID WITH SILVER RIVETS
The finished piece with inlaid silver rivets running along its length.

CERAMIC BEADS AND PENDANTS

CLAY OCCURS NATURALLY; IT IS COMPOSED OF FINE-GRAINED MINERALS AND, DEPENDING ON ITS WATER CONTENT, HAS A CERTAIN PLASTICITY. MOULDED, THROWN OR COILED PIECES CAN BE LEFT TO DRY AND HARDEN AND ARE THEN FIRED AND GLAZED TO PRODUCE A DURABLE, HARDWEARING MATERIAL THAT CAN BE USED TO MAKE HOUSEHOLD GOODS – POTS, VASES, PLATES, CUPS, TILES AND SO ON. IT IS ALSO USED IN INDUSTRY FOR MAKING PIPES, TILES AND OTHER BUILDING MATERIALS.

There are several kinds of clay, but for the purposes of making jewellery pieces, you can use either stoneware clay or earthenware clay. Check the firing temperature for your clay – choose one that fires to temperatures between 1000 and 1080ºC (1800 and 2000ºF).

Clay is malleable, which makes it the ideal medium for rolling, throwing and modeling, and it can be used to make beads and clay jewellery. Pieces are dried and fired in a 'bisque firing'. This is the name given to the first firing which makes the clay more durable for handling, but leaves it porous enough to take added colour and glaze.

TOOLS AND MATERIALS

CLAY

ROLLING PIN

BOARD

RULER

CRAFT KNIFE

KNITTING NEEDLE OR TOOTHPICK

WOODEN TOOL OR SPONGE

CRAFT KNIFE

SANDPAPER

DUST MASK

KILN

SMALL PAINTBRUSH

UNDERGLAZE COLOUR

GLAZE

KANTHAL WIRE

TUBE-SHAPED BEADS

1 STARTING OFF
Break off a small piece of clay.

2 MAKING A SLAB
Roll the clay out evenly using a rolling pin on a board.

Underglaze colours are commercially available colours that can be bought in powder form or in premixed tubes. They are water-based and can be mixed to create your own colour range. They can be painted onto bisque-fired pieces. A glaze is then applied to the piece, and it is fired again to finish.

Glazes can be purchased in powder form in small quantities, ready to be mixed with water. Choose a transparent, low-firing glaze to apply to your pieces after you have painted them with underglaze colours. Coloured glazes are also available for single-coloured beads and pendants; the application process for both types of glaze is the same. These fire to various temperatures, and you should check with your glaze supplier before firing.

You can make beads and pendants by hand from coils of clay or from solid balls of clay. Use a needle or a toothpick to push a hole through the balls of clay or through pieces that have been rolled out and cut.

3 CUTTING STRIPS
Cut strips of clay using a ruler and a craft knife to get a straight edge. Carefully lift the strips individually.

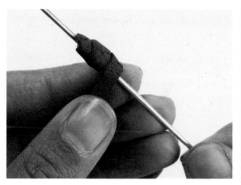

4 COILING THE STRIPS
Coil each strip carefully around a knitting needle or a toothpick.

6 FINISHING OFF
To reshape the coil, roll it gently on a board with the knitting needle or toothpick still inside.

PORCELAIN BROOCH
by Daisy Choi
This porcelain brooch is set with a gemstone and has a crackle-glaze finish and a diamond graphic. It is attached to a moving silver ball and chain.

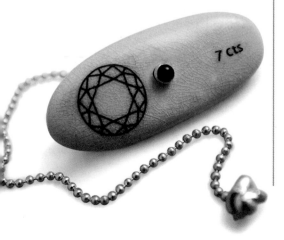

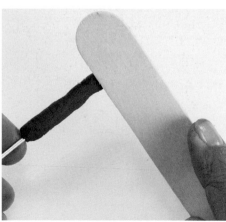

5 SMOOTHING THE COIL
Smooth the edges of the coil using a dampened finger or a wooden tool or sponge, to form a neat tube of clay.

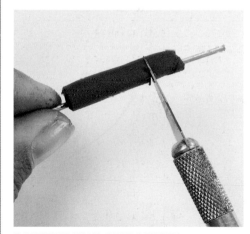

7 CUTTING YOUR BEAD LENGTH
Use a sharp craft knife to cut the tube into the lengths you want, twisting the needle as you cut, and then leave them to dry.

PORCELAIN RING

by Daisy Choi

This ring is made from porcelain with a crackle glaze and mounted onto an oxidized silver ring.

ROUND BEADS

1 ROLLING ROUND BEADS

Take a small piece of clay – the same size as for a tube-shaped bead. Roll the piece of clay in the palm of your hands, applying slight pressure to achieve the desired shape.

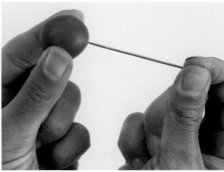
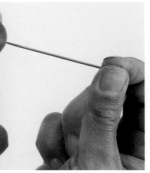

2 MAKING THE HOLE

Hold the bead carefully in one hand and pierce it through with a toothpick or a sharp tool to make a hole. At this stage you could also use a sharp tool or a toothpick to incise a pattern onto the surface of your bead.

FLAT SHAPES

1 CUTTING SHAPES

Roll out a slab of clay. Use a craft knife to cut out shapes. At this stage you could also incise a pattern onto the shapes using a pin or wooden craft tool. Make a hole on one side of each shape using a pin. Leave the pieces to dry, turning them over occasionally so that they don't curl up.

2 DRYING TO LEATHER HARD

Place all your beads on a flat surface and leave them to dry until they are leather hard. You will know when this has happened because the colour of the clay will change.

3 SANDING AND FINISHING

At the leather-hard stage, sand each piece with a coarse sandpaper for an even surface. Wear a dust mask and handle the pieces carefully as they are very delicate at this stage.

FIRING AND GLAZING

1 BISQUE FIRING

When your pieces are thoroughly dry (the clay changes colour when dry and becomes much paler), fire them in a kiln to the recommended temperature. The pieces shown here have been bisque fired and are ready to decorate.

2 MIXING UNDERGLAZE COLOUR

Mix glaze to the consistency of single cream and store it in a jar with a lid. Underglaze colours come in tubes but might need to be mixed with a little water. They can also be mixed together to make new colours.

3 USING UNDERGLAZE COLOUR

Hold the shape carefully in one hand and use a small paintbrush to paint patterns onto your bisque-fired piece with an underglaze colour. Bisque-fired clay is porous and the underglaze colours will dry almost as soon as you apply them. When the first coat has dried, apply a second coat to achieve a good depth of colour. You can paint different colours on top of each other. Handle pieces with care as they dry.

4 GLAZING

Thread your beads onto a toothpick or needle and carefully brush the glaze onto them. Do the same to your flat pieces, painting both sides. Make sure that you don't block the threading hole through the beads, push a pin through to keep the hole clear. Glazed pieces can be handled with care when dry.

Tips

- *Wrap clay in damp cloth even while you are using it. When you have finished for the day, wrap it in polythene as well. Leave it in a cool place.*
- *If clay does dry out, it can be reconstituted with water.*
- *Cover pieces in progress with a damp cloth and polythene, so that you can continue to work on them later if necessary.*

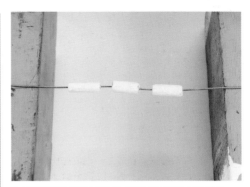

5 PACKING THE KILN AND GLAZE FIRING

Thread your beads carefully onto Kanthal wire (available from ceramic supply stores). Balance the wire ends on kiln props so that the beads and pendants are threaded and hanging on the wire but not touching each other or the sides or bottom of the kiln. Glaze is liquid glass, and if they are touching, they will fuse together. Fire at the temperature recommended by the glaze supplier and wait for the kiln to cool before you remove your work.

6 FINISHED BEADS

The finished beads were painted with an underglaze, glazed, and then fired.

GLASS

GLASS JEWELLERY IS NOT ONLY FAIRLY SIMPLE TO MAKE BUT CAN BE VERY EFFECTIVE, AS IT CAPTURES AND REFLECTS THE LIGHT SO WELL. OTHER THAN ACCESS TO A SMALL KILN, THE MOST IMPORTANT THING YOU NEED IS A STEADY HAND, AS ASSEMBLING THE PIECE FOR FIRING CAN BE AN INTRICATE JOB.

The fusing technique used to make glass jewellery involves layering coloured glass pieces together on a kiln shelf and heating them to a temperature of around 800°C (1470°F). Various ranges of specialist fusing glass are available. This glass is generally sold in the form of coloured sheets, as well as other forms that can be used to add decorative effects. These include glass powders and granules known as 'frits', long thin strips of glass known as 'noodles' and 'stringers', and paper-thin fragments of glass called 'confetti'. To achieve successful fusing results, it is crucial to use compatible glass – in other words, to use products from only one specialist range.

The hotter the glass goes in the kiln – up to 830°C (1520°F) – the more rounded and deformed its edges will become. The same is true for any decorative pieces added on top, which will melt into the layers below to give a totally smooth top surface. However, to retain some texture and edge definition, try experimenting in the lower temperature ranges – 770–800°C (1420–1470°F). Remember that glass can be heated more than once in the kiln, so a useful tip is to create a smooth base for your jewellery in a very hot firing and then add the decorative elements and refire at a lower temperature, according to the effect you are after.

TOOLS AND MATERIALS

GLASS CUTTER

STRAIGHTEDGE

GLASS

OLD TOWEL

KILN

CERAMIC FIBRE PAPER

CRAFT GLUE

COPPER OR NICHROTHAL WIRE

DUST MASK

NEWSPAPER

KILN
To fuse glass, you will need a small kiln with a flat kiln shelf.

ASSEMBLING A BASIC CABOCHON

1 PREPARATION
You will need a glass cutter (a pistol-grip cutter is shown here, but there are many different types) and a straightedge. Ensure that your glass cutter has been filled with oil to lubricate it and aid cutting. You will also need access to a small kiln with a flat kiln shelf on which to arrange your work.

2 SCORING THE GLASS
You will be scoring a line into the glass with the glass cutter; you can either use a ruler or work freehand. Work from edge to edge and never stop the scoreline midway across the glass. Push down fairly hard as you draw the cutter along the edge so that you can hear the cutter scoring the line into the surface of the glass.

When you are working with small pieces of glass – less than 5cm (2in) square – these rules can be relaxed. With very tiny pieces it is even possible just to switch on the kiln to its highest setting and switch it off once the top temperature has been reached. If your kiln has various settings, it is worth incorporating an annealing stage into your firing to ensure against cracking the glass: Ask your supplier for the annealing temperature of your glass and hold the temperature steady for about fifteen minutes at this point.

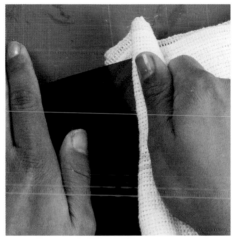

3 BREAKING ALONG THE LINE

If you have produced a good score line, running from one edge of the glass to the other, you should be able to break the glass cleanly and easily along it. Turn the glass over so that the score line faces down. Using a towel to protect your hands, break the glass away from you by pressing down. You can use this scoring and breaking method to cut any straight-sided shape from glass. But remember you must always work from one edge of the glass to the other, so you may have to make two or three cuts to get the shape you want.

4 PREPARING TO FIRE

Make sure your pieces of glass are totally clean before placing them in the kiln. You will need a piece of ceramic fibre paper slightly larger than your glass to prevent it from adhering to the kiln shelf in the firing process. A very fine fibre paper will ensure the glass has a totally smooth underside.

5 MAKING A CABOCHON

Two layers of glass will produce a nice chunky fused nugget of glass known as a 'cabochon'. These need to be properly aligned to produce smooth rounded edges; use a small dot of craft glue to hold the layers together. The glue should burn away when used sparingly – excessive glue will leave a residue.

6 THE FINISHED CABOCHON

After fusing, the two green squares of glass have fused into a lovely rounded nugget. The fibre paper will have turned into a powdery substance that must be disposed of very carefully. Wearing a dust mask, scrape the powder off the kiln shelf and onto a piece of newspaper, which can then be wrapped up and thrown away. Do this slowly to avoid creating harmful airborne particles. You could now take this nugget and add decoration (see page 129).

THE FIRING CYCLE

The firing cycle for fusing glass usually involves various stages where the glass must be heated at different rates to retain its integrity. The principles of glass fusing involve heating the glass up slowly and evenly to around 540°C (1000°F) to avoid thermal shock and then heating as fast as possible up to the top temperature. When cooling the glass, the most important temperature is known as the 'annealing point', and this varies depending on the type of glass used. Once cooled to this point, the kiln must be held at this temperature for a certain length of time (dependent on the size of the glass), and this annealing period will relieve all internal tensions in the glass and prevent the glass from shattering. After this, the glass should be cooled slowly to room temperature before being removed from the kiln.

MAKING A FUSED-GLASS PENDANT

FINISHED PENDANTS

You can make many pendants or cabochons in one firing, as long as there is at least 1.5cm (½in) space around each one. The smaller the shapes or the hotter the temperature they reach in the kiln, the more they will deform and round off. Pieces like these can form the basis of your glass jewellery and can be added to and decorated further.

1 PREPARING THE PENDANT

If you are making a pendant, this is the stage to consider how you will hang the glass. You can incorporate a loop of wire between two layers of glass so that the ends will be trapped inside the fused glass. Copper wire will work, but nichrothal wire is especially suitable, as it keeps its strength at high temperatures.

2 MAKING A CHANNEL THROUGH A PENDANT

It is possible to make a pendant with a channel through it through which to thread a leather thong. Roll a piece of fibre paper around a length of wire and sandwich it between two layers of glass, ensuring you've left a good seam of glass either side of the wire. The fibre paper will prevent the glass from fusing together, and it can be pulled out after cooling to leave a channel through the glass.

DECORATIVE EFFECTS

1 FRITS, STRINGERS AND NOODLES

As long as you use compatible glass, from the same range as for the body of your piece, there are many products on the market that can be used for decorative effects. These include frits, stringers, noodles and confetti. These can be added at any stage in the making process, but bear in mind that if they are included in the first firing, they will become fully fused into the glass base and go completely flat.

Tip
Once your fused-glass pieces are finished, you can glue jewellery bails to the back of the fused glass to make necklaces or earrings. You could also make cufflinks, rings and brooches. Use a two-part epoxy glue suitable for glass to ensure your jewellery is long-lasting.

2 ADDING A GLASS NOODLE

Before the first firing, you may like to add decorative accents, such as a length of glass noodle (as shown here), to provide a contrasting colour accent. Glass noodles can be broken by hand or scored with the glass cutter and snapped. You may find it easier to manipulate small fragments of glass with a pair of tweezers. Any larger pieces will need a dot of glue to keep them in place, but wait until the glue is dry before firing. Here you can see a glass pendant before (above) and after (below) firing.

3 PIECES AFTER THE FIRST FIRING

It's difficult to add many layers of decoration in one firing, as the tiny pieces won't hold together, so a series of low-temperature firings can work well. After adding the first layer of decoration to your glass cabochons, you can refire them at a lower temperature to retain some texture and surface sparkle in the decorations, as you can see in the pieces pictured here.

THE FINISHED CABOCHONS

After the final firing, the decoration on these cabochons has fused right into the glass base to give the cabochons completely smooth surfaces.

CONCRETE

A CONCRETE MIXTURE CAN BE PACKED INTO A MOULD OR INTO TWO METAL SHAPES TO MAKE JEWELLERY PIECES.

The use of concrete in jewellery making is unusual, but the ease with which it can be cast and the variety of surface textures and colours that can be created make it an effective material for jewellery making.

Concrete is a dry material that is made by combining cement, sand and water. These are mixed together to form a hard material, and additives such as metal findings, polypropylene fibres, stone dust and gravel can be added to the mixture to enhance its appearance, increase strength and reduce shrinkage.

Concrete contrasts well with precious metals such as silver or gold. It can be applied within a fabricated structure or cast into a mould for more sculptural pieces.

TOOLS AND MATERIALS

CEMENT

SAND

WATER

MOULD

TOOL FOR LEVELLING

SHEET OF PLASTIC

BASIC CONCRETE TECHNIQUES

1 MEASURING MATERIALS
Measure the cement, sand and water. The proportions may vary according to the additives.

2 MIXING
Mix the dry materials together in a mixing bowl.

4 PACKING THE MOULD
If you are using a plaster mould, apply a release agent to the inside of the mould to seal the surface and soak the mould in water for a few minutes. Plaster is very absorbent, and it would otherwise absorb the moisture from the mixture too quickly. Use a spoon or spatula to pack the mixture into the mould. Add the mixture in batches and pack it well.

Tip
Soak a plaster mould in water before using it.

3 ADDING WATER
Add water to the dry materials and mix until all the water has been absorbed.

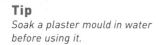

5 LEVELLING THE MIXTURE
Pack the mixture so that it is level with the top of the mould. Use a tool to scrape the top to ensure it is completely level.

6 TAPPING THE MOULD
Tap the mould lightly to compact the mixture further and to help release it from the surface of the mould.

7 COVERING THE MOULD
Cover the mould with a sheet of plastic to keep it from drying out too quickly. If the concrete loses moisture too quickly, it will weaken the material. Hardening can take up to forty-eight hours; however it depends on the size of the piece.

8 REMOVING THE PIECE FROM THE MOULD
Remove the hardened piece from the mould. If it is hardened, the concrete will have changed colour.

SILVER BANGLE SET WITH CONCRETE
After twenty-four hours, the concrete will have hardened, and the bangle can be finished as usual.

METAL AND CONCRETE

1 USING A METAL CASING
This example shows a silver bangle that will be packed with concrete between the gaps. A copper wire has been soldered between the two bands of silver to help secure the concrete mixture.

2 PACKING IN THE CONCRETE
Place the metal on a sheet of plastic and pack the concrete mixture between the gaps. Push the mixture to the bottom of the gap so that it is flush on the other side.

3 LEVELLING THE CONCRETE
Use a flat-edged tool to level the surface of the concrete. Cover with a sheet of plastic and leave it to harden for twenty-four hours.

CHAPTER 6

CASTING

NECKLACE *(opposite)*
by Sarah King
Mixed blue ovals made from bioresin,
an eco-plastic, make up this necklace.

STRAWBERRY NECKLACE *(left)*
by Tina Lilienthal
Cast resin skulls and strawberries are
joined with silver for this necklace.

CUFFLINKS *(right)*
by Melissa Hansom
These cufflinks were decorated with
resin, coloured blue and poured into
rectangular silver tubing.

WING RING *(top right)*
by Burcu Buyukunal
Ring constructed from cast epoxy
resin wings and a cast sterling
silver ring shank.

Resin is liquid plastic that requires a hardener for curing to
a firm material. Resin can be cast in a number of ways to
make jewellery. This chapter takes you step by step through
the different casting processes and provides advice on
decision making when it comes to choosing materials for
mould and master making.

CASTING PROPERTIES

CASTING IS A TECHNIQUE THAT CAN BE USED TO MAKE MULTIPLES OF THE SAME MASTER. THERE ARE A NUMBER OF MATERIALS THAT CAN BE USE FOR CASTING; THE CHOICE DEPENDS ON THE RESULTS YOU DESIRE. SOME CASTING MATERIALS INCLUDE RESIN, SILICONE AND PLASTER.

Resin is liquid plastic that can be poured into a mould and cured to a hard material. The liquid plastic is transformed into a solid material by adding a catalyst. The hardened plastic can be sanded and polished to finish. Resin can be dyed a large range of colours, and items can be embedded into the resin.

Silicone is liquid rubber that is used for making moulds, and any shape can be copied. The range of silicones available is vast, and they can vary in flexibility and durability. Choosing the correct silicone for the job is partly about experimenting with different types of silicone and partly about deciding whether you require a flexible or a

PLASTER	WAX	POLYMER CLAY

rigid mould. A flexible silicone mould is best for casting resin because the resin can be easily removed from the mould.

Plaster is a powder mixed with water to make a hard material that can be carved and shaped. It can be used to make a positive piece that can be copied or to make a negative mould. It is the preferred material for experimentation because it is fast drying and inexpensive.

DESIGNING WITH CASTING

Qualities Casting materials can be flexible and firm, and can produce copies of very detailed designs. The fast-drying nature of plaster is ideal for quick prototyping, whereas most resins take a week or longer.

Applications Resin is used for making finished pieces of jewellery, while plaster is used for either prototyping or mould making. Silicone is used for making moulds and for casting jewellery pieces. Pigments can be added to resin to enhance the colour of its appearance.

Combining with other materials Most materials can be copied either in plaster or silicone to make a mould and multiple copies. The easiest material to copy is wax because the surface does not require a release agent, and it can be shaped and carved effortlessly.

Where to look for inspiration
• **Carla Edwards, United Kingdom**
www.carlaedwards.pwp.blueyonder.co.uk
Resin jewellery, focusing on pattern and colour.
• **Mari Ishikawa, Germany**
www.mari-ishikawa.de/index.htm
Cast metal and mixed media, based on botanical forms.
• **Melanie Bilenker, United States**
www.melaniebilenker.com
Jewellery using hair as a drawing media, in resin.

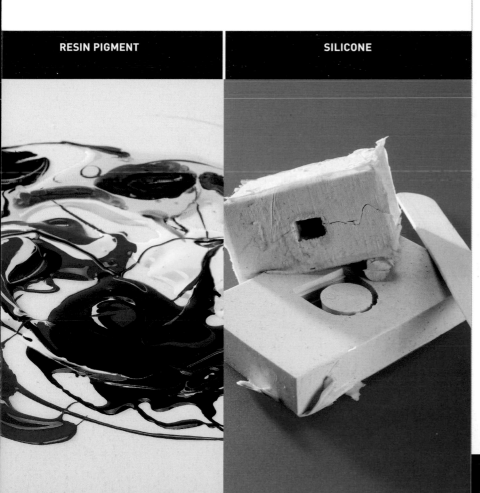

RESIN PIGMENT

SILICONE

RESIN

RESIN IS LIQUID PLASTIC THAT CAN BE CAST INTO ANY SHAPE. PIGMENTS CAN BE ADDED TO IT TO ACHIEVE A RANGE OF BEAUTIFUL COLOURS.

The liquid plastic is transformed into a solid material by adding a catalyst. Once set, this solid plastic can be cut, carved and polished. Once the catalyst is added to the resin the curing process starts, and the resin will become warm. There are many types of resins, and each has its own properties and applications. It is important to refer to the manufacturer's data sheet when purchasing and preparing resin. Each type of resin is prepared differently, with a varying percentage of catalyst to resin. It is very important to follow the mixing instructions correctly because improper mixing can result in poor casting.

Epoxy resin is ideal for casting jewellery pieces, and all the demonstrations in this section were cast with epoxy resin. Polyester resin is also suitable for jewellery making and is ideal for bigger pieces such as bracelets. It is best to experiment with a few types of resins and select the one that produces the best results for you. Keep accurate notes while experimenting so that you can repeat what you have done.

⚠ HEALTH AND SAFETY

Health and safety are highly important when you are working with resins. Resins are toxic and can have associated health risks. Read the manufacturer's instructions before using any products. Wear a good face mask that protects against fumes, as well as rubber gloves. Only work in a well-ventilated area. Resins are strong-smelling and produce toxic fumes, so keep them away from children. Prolonged exposure without proper safety protection can have serious health implications. If resin comes into contact with skin, it can cause irritation. Wash immediately with a handwash suitable for resin.

FLEXIBLE RESIN MOULDS

Silicone or rubber make the best moulds for pouring resin. The resin cures into a solid plastic, and a flexible mould will allow the resin to be removed easily. Some plastic packaging can be used for casting, such as chocolate boxes or water bottles. Some packaging will be stamped on the bottom, identifying the type of plastic used; any stamped with PE (polyethylene) or PP (polypropylene) would be suitable.

PIGMENTS

There are two main types of pigments: opaque and transparent. Pigments can be mixed together to create a range of colours and then added to the resin mixture. You only need a small amount; if you add too much, it can prevent curing.

EMBEDDING OBJECTS

Objects can be embedded in resin, but bear in mind that organic material may discolour it over time. If the embedded objects are too big, they may prevent the resin from curing fully, and it will remain tacky. Objects such as thread, beads and plastic pieces can all be embedded successfully.

USING RESIN WITH METAL SHAPES

Resin can be poured into premade metal shapes; it will adhere to the metal, but it is worth keying the surface by rubbing with sandpaper before pouring the resin.

FINISHING RESIN CASTINGS

Full curing takes at least a week; when fully cured, the resin surface should feel hard. However, on some occasions, the surface will remain tacky, but the tacky surface can be sanded off. In general, casting done in an open mould will need to be sanded to a smooth finish with wet and dry sandpaper. If the surface is uneven and requires lots of sanding, start with a coarse paper and use every grade of paper to the finest. A little water can be added to the paper for a smooth matt finish. The pieces can then be highly polished on a polishing motor (see polishing plastic, page 53).

CAST-RESIN SHAPES

These cast-resin shapes were made from an ice-cube tray. A hole can be drilled, and they can be used as pendants.

TOOLS AND MATERIALS

FACE MASK

RUBBER GLOVES

PLASTIC MIXING CUP

SCALES

MIXING STICKS

FLEXIBLE OPEN MOULD

CLOSED MOULD

RUBBER BANDS

TAPE

JEWELLERY SAW

FILES

SANDPAPER

METAL PIECES

SCULPTING CLAY

Tips
- Keep accurate notes when mixing pigments so that you can repeat the colour. Pouring two different colours at the same time will produce a two-tone cast.
- There is no need to buy lots of colours. Buy the primary colours (red, yellow and blue) as well as black and white, and from these you can create a range of other colours.

WORKING WITH RESIN

1 PREPARING RESIN

Resin can be mixed by weight or by parts; however, follow the mixing instructions for the product you are using. You can use special plastic mixing cups or any plastic container marked with PE or PP on the bottom. If you are mixing by weight, place the mixing cup on the scales, pour the resin into the container and then add the hardener.

2 MIXING THE RESIN

Mix the resin thoroughly but not too vigorously. Avoid adding too much air to the mixture because this may cause air bubbles.

3 MIXING PIGMENT

Add a small amount of pigment to the mixture. Remember that too much pigment can prevent the resin from curing. You can mix pigments in a separate container until you get the desired colour.

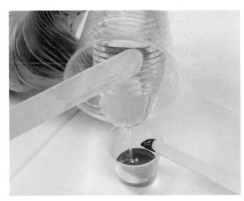

4 ADDING PIGMENT

Once you have the desired colour, add the resin mixture to the pigment. Mix the pigment thoroughly with the resin. To avoid getting streaks, it may be best to use a new mixing stick.

5 POURING RESIN INTO AN OPEN MOULD

First, place the mould on a level surface. Pour the mixture into the cavity and fill to the top. If some mixture spills over the edge of the cavity, remove it with a paper towel or it can be sanded flat once cured. Pour the resin into a flexible mould, such as a silicone or rubber mould. Ice-cube trays make excellent moulds.

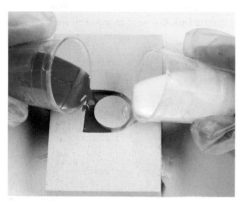

6 POURING TWO COLOURS

For a two-toned piece of jewellery, pour both resin mixtures simultaneously, and the colours will fill to the top of the mould but remain separate. The two-tone effect can also be achieved by filling one half of the cavity with one colour, allowing it to set for an hour and then pouring the second colour on top.

USING A CLOSED MOULD

1 SECURING A CLOSED MOULD

Before using a closed mould, secure the sides with a rubber band to keep the resin from leaking out.

2 POURING RESIN INTO A CLOSED MOULD

Pour the resin into the sprue hole and fill the mould to the top. If resin begins to leak out from the sides, secure them with tape.

3 THE CAST PIECES

The finished cast will have a sprue that can be removed with a jewellery saw. It may also have a seam that can be filed or sanded. In the examples above, the piece on the left is the cast resin with the sprue removed, and on the right is the wooden master used to make the silicone mould (see Casting with a wood master, page 145).

EMBEDDING

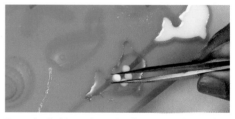

To embed objects in resin, first, pour the resin mixture into a mould. In this example, a flexible rubber ice-cube tray is being used as a mould dish. It is best to use a plain resin mixture or one that has a very small amount of transparent pigment. Use a pair of tweezers to place the objects to be embedded in the resin. Objects will sink to the bottom of the mould dish. If you want them to sit in the middle, fill half the mould with resin and leave it to cure for one or two hours. Place the objects onto the partly cured mixture and pour a new batch of the same resin over the top.

POURING RESIN INTO METAL

1 POURING THE RESIN

Key the metal surface with sandpaper. The resin mixture can be poured directly, or for small areas, use a mixing stick to apply it. Fill the shape so the resin is slightly raised above the surface of the metal. (As the resin cures it will shrink.)

2 SCULPTING CLAY

Resin can also be poured into the gaps between two pieces of metal. Key the inner surfaces of the metal. Place the shapes on a sheet of plastic that the resin will not adhere to. Use sculpting clay to seal the bottom. Try not to get the clay inside the shape because it will stick to the resin and create a hole when it hardens.

3 POURING THE RESIN

Pour the resin slowly. If it starts to leak from the bottom, stop, adjust the sculpting material, and then continue pouring.

FINISHED RESIN RING

This ring had different-coloured resins poured into shaped settings.

RESIN NECKLACE
by Tina Lilienthal

The strawberries and skulls incorporated into this necklace were cast in polyester resin and linked with silver, including detailed silver stalks on the strawberries.

FINISHED RESIN PENDANT

Resin was poured into the gaps between these circlets of silver, and a hole was left empty in the centre.

SILICONE MOULD MAKING

THERE ARE TWO TYPES OF MOULD: OPEN AND CLOSED. OPEN MOULDS ARE OPEN ON ONE SIDE AND CLOSED MOULDS ARE ENCLOSED WITH A SMALL POURING HOLE. BOTH TYPES CAN BE USED MANY TIMES FOR CASTING.

A mould can be a negative or a positive form that is used to cast multiples of the same object. Liquid material can be poured into a negative mould and, once cured, a positive form is released. Moulds can be made from silicone or plaster. The choice of mould-making materials depends on what will be cast. For casting resin, a silicone mould is the most suitable; however, a plaster mould can also be used for casting resin (see Making a plaster mould, page 143).

SILICONE

Silicone is liquid rubber that requires a hardener to 'cure' into a solid material. The correct ratio of hardener to silicone is necessary to aid perfect curing; this can be measured by weight or in parts. Always follow the manufacturer's instructions.

The range of silicones available is vast, and they can vary in flexibility and durability. Choosing the correct silicone for the job is partly about experimenting with different types of silicone and partly about deciding whether you require a flexible or a rigid mould. A flexible silicone mould is best for casting resin because the resin can be easily removed from the mould.

OPEN MOULD

Open moulds have one open side into which casting materials can be poured. Ready-made mould dishes can be purchased from art stores and are usually made from plastic, but a mould dish can be made from sheets of plastic or cardboard. It should have four walls and a base, sealed at the seams. The bottom of the mould dish will become the top of the mould once cured, so clean and smooth materials should be used to ensure a good surface. When making an open mould, remember that the sides of the mould dish must be straight or at a slight outwards angle to allow for easy release. Don't angle the wall inwards because this will make it difficult to release the mould after curing. The master – the piece being copied – needs to have one flat side so it can sit flush with the surface of the mould dish. This type of mould is ideal for simple shapes.

CLOSED MOULD

A closed mould is completely enclosed, with a small pouring hole (a sprue). The sprue is made by attaching a piece of wood or metal to one end of the master. A wall is built around the master with cardboard or plastic sheets, and all joints are sealed with a glue gun or sculpting clay. Silicone is poured into the walls, over the master and, when cured, the walls are removed. The silicone is cut halfway down the middle to release the master. This type of mould is ideal for an organic-shaped master with uneven sides.

OPEN SILICONE MOULD

TOOLS AND MATERIALS
MASTER
PVA GLUE
MOULD DISH
SILICONE AND HARDENER
SCALES
MIXING STICKS
FIRM CARDBOARD OR SHEET PLASTIC
GLUE GUN OR SOFT SCULPTING CLAY
SHARP CRAFT KNIFE

1 PLACING THE MASTER
Apply a thin layer of PVA glue to the flat side of the master. Place it in the middle of the mould dish, with the glue side facing down. Leave it to dry for a few minutes. Note: If you are using a wooden master (see page 145) you will need to apply a release agent before it can be used for making a mould. Wax masters do not require a release agent.

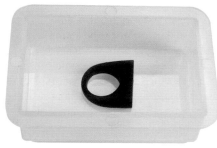

2 SEALING EDGES

Make sure the edges of the master make full contact with the surface of the mould dish. If there are any gaps, the silicone will seep under the master, and the surface of the mould will be uneven.

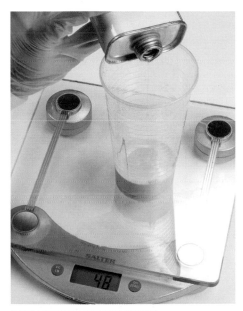

3 MEASURING THE SILICONE AND HARDENER

Mix the silicone with the hardener, following the manufacturer's mixing instructions. It is advisable to use a flexible silicone for easy removal of cast objects. You can mix by weight or by parts; if you mix by weight, set the scale to zero, measure the silicone, and then add the hardener.

4 MIXING THE SILICONE AND HARDENER

Mix the silicone with the hardener thoroughly but not too vigorously, to avoid air bubbles getting into the mixture.

5 POURING THE MIXTURE OVER THE MOULD

Pour the mixture over the master until it is completely covered, with 12mm (½in) above the master. Air bubbles may rise to the surface; tapping the mould dish lightly will encourage more air bubbles to rise.

Tip

If you are mixing large amounts of silicone, such as 1kg (2lb), use a large mixing dish and mix the hardener thoroughly with the silicone.

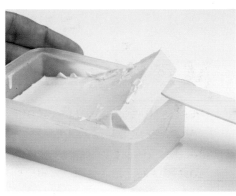

6 REMOVING THE MOULD

Depending on the silicone you are using, it may take between four and twenty-four hours to harden or cure. Once hardened, it will feel firm and rubbery. Remove it from the dish by prying away the edges.

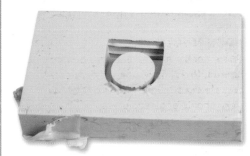

7 THE FINISHED OPEN MOULD

The finished mould should be completely solid. If areas of the mould have not set, it may need a bit longer. It's also possible that the percentage of hardener to silicone was incorrect, or the mixture was not mixed thoroughly enough.

CLOSED SILICONE MOULD

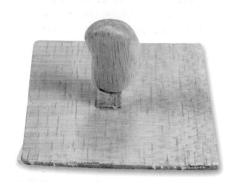

1 MAKING THE SPRUE
The master should have a rod attached to its base, called a 'sprue', which will become the pouring hole for the resin. The sprue can be attached with a screw or glued. If you are using a wood master, it should be scratch-free and sealed with a release agent.

2 MAKING A MOULD DISH
Build a wall around the master with firm pieces of cardboard or acrylic sheets. The wall should pull away easily once the silicone is cured. Leave a 6mm (¼in) space around the master. Secure the corners with a glue gun or soft sculpting clay. Ensure that the edges are sealed, or the silicone will leak during pouring. Mix the silicone (see Steps 3, 4 and 5 for open mould) and pour it over the master.

3 THE FINISHED CLOSED MOULD
Once the silicone is cured, remove the walls.

4 CUTTING THE MOULD
Hold the mould with the sprue facing up and, with a sharp craft knife, cut from the sprue down the sides. Don't cut all the way to the bottom because that's where the mould should be connected.

5 REMOVING THE MASTER
It should be easy to remove the master from the mould. If it doesn't come away easily, cut a bit farther down the sides. Once the master has been removed, the mould can be used. Tie the sides with a rubber band and pour resin into the sprue hole.

FINISHED CAST-RESIN PENDANT
The finished pendant has been cast in red resin and mounted on a chain.

PLASTER MOULDS

CASTING PLASTER IS A WHITE POWDER THAT IS MIXED WITH WATER TO FORM A THICK PASTE THAT SETS SOLID. IT CAN BE USED TO MAKE MOULDS FOR CASTING RESIN, CONCRETE, CERAMICS SILICONE AND A NUMBER OF OTHER MATERIALS.

A release agent must be used when the mould is made so that the master of the object to be copied can be removed from the mould once it is set. A release agent also needs to be applied to the mould before it is used to make a casting. Vaseline, wax, and varnish are common release agents, but the type of release agent depends on the material used for the mould and for the casting.

TOOLS AND MATERIALS

CARDBOARD

MASKING TAPE

WAX MASTER (SEE PAGE 146)

MIXING BOWL

PLASTER

WATER

SPATULA

METAL RULER

RELEASE AGENT

PAINTBRUSH

Tip
Before pouring plaster into a mould, mark a line on the inside of the mould so you know how much plaster to pour.

MAKING A SIMPLE MOULD

1 MAKING A BOX
Make a box from cardboard and masking tape. It should have an open top and be big enough to fit the master with at least 6mm (¼in) space around it.

2 SETTING UP
Place the master with the flat side down in the centre of the box. In this example the master is made from wax.

OPEN MOULD
The simplest way to achieve a casting is to use an open mould made with casting plaster. A box is made, and the edges secured to prevent plaster from leaking out. The box should be made with a material that is easy to remove from the plaster once it is cured, and cardboard is the ideal material for this job. The cardboard needs to be firm so it can maintain its shape while the plaster is poured.

WAX MASTER
The master used to make a plaster mould should be completely flat on one side, and the sides should be tapered by at least three degrees. The tapered sides are very important to allow the master to release from the mould easily. Wax (see also page 146) is a good material to use for a master. It is easy to carve, a smooth surface can be achieved easily and it does not require a release agent as wood masters do.

In the example on these pages, a wax master is used; however, if you use another material, such as wood, then apply a release agent. When mixing plaster, you should always add the plaster to the water and mix thoroughly. Air bubbles will begin to form in the plaster, and these can be removed by tapping the mixing container. The bubbles will rise to the surface and disappear.

▶

3 MIXING THE PLASTER

Fill a container half full of water and add small batches of plaster to the water until the mixture has a thick consistency. The amount of plaster mixture you need depends on the size of the mould you are making.

5 POURING THE PLASTER

Pour the mixture into the mould to cover the master by at least 6mm (¼in). Set aside and leave it to harden. You will know it is hardened when the plaster feels firm to the touch and has changed colour. The hardening time depends on how big the mould is and the temperature of the air.

7 REVEALING THE MASTER

Turn the mould over and the master should be visible. If there is plaster around the edges of the master, use a metal ruler to scrape off the excess plaster. The edges of the master should be visible. Release the master from the mould by tapping lightly on the back. If the master does not come out, check that all the edges are revealed.

4 STIRRING THE PLASTER

Stir the plaster until you have a smooth and lump-free mixture. It should be thick but runny. Tap the container lightly to allow trapped air bubbles to rise to the surface before pouring the plaster.

6 REMOVING THE BOX

Remove the box from around the plaster. A thin layer of cardboard may be stuck to the plaster, and this can be scraped off.

8 APPLYING RELEASE AGENT

Before using the mould, brush release agent on the inside of the mould. You may need to apply several coats depending on the particular solution. Follow the instructions of the solution you are using. The mould is now ready to use.

CASTING WITH A WOOD MASTER

WOOD IS IDEALLY SUITED TO MAKING A MASTER, AS IT EASY TO WORK WITH AND WIDELY AVAILABLE IN MOST ART SHOPS AND TIMBER YARDS.

TOOLS AND MATERIALS

BLOCK OF WOOD

PENCIL

JEWELLERY SAW

BLADES

FACE MASK

LARGE FLAT FILE

NEEDLE FILES

SANDPAPER

WOOD GLUE

RELEASE AGENT

COTTON SWAB

Wood is ideal for prototyping designs because it is inexpensive and easy to work with. It is best to use a soft wood such as balsa for carving. Blocks of wood can be cut with a jewellery saw or bandsaw, and thin sheets can be cut with a sharp craft knife. Once the master is carved, the surface can be sanded with fine sandpaper. The process is the same whether you are making a master for a closed or an open mould.

MASTER FOR A CLOSED MOULD

Any organic-shaped master needs a closed mould, and a mould of this type needs to have a sprue (see page 142). The sprue is made by attaching either a wooden or metal rod to one end of the master, the rod is then attached to the bottom of the mould surface and a wall is built around the master. In the finished mould, the master is removed along with the rod, and the bottom of the mould becomes the top with a hole.

MASTER FOR AN OPEN MOULD

A master for an open mould needs to have a flat side. The flat side is attached to the mould dish, so it's important that it's completely flat, otherwise silicone will seep under the edges and create an uneven surface on the mould. Sanding or filing the wood can achieve a really flat surface.

1 CUTTING
Draw your design on the wood with a pencil. Insert a metal cutting blade into the jewellery saw and cut around the design (see page 22). Wood produces lots of dust during cutting and filing so you should always wear a face mask.

2 SHAPING
Using a large coarse flat file, shape the wood following your design. This may take some time to achieve. Use needle files for smaller shapes.

3 SANDING THE SURFACE
Once you have the basic shape, sand the surface with a coarse sandpaper to remove any file marks. Work towards finer grades of sandpaper for a smooth finish.

4 MAKING THE SPRUE
Cut a small shape out of wood to fit the bottom of the master. Use a wood glue to attach it – this is called the 'sprue'. The sprue can also be screwed onto the master.

5 APPLYING RELEASE AGENT
In order for the master to release easily from the mould, you must apply a release agent to the surface with a cotton swab. There are a few types of release agents available, and most art shops can suggest the best one to use on wood.

CASTING WITH A WAX MASTER

WAX IS AN EXCELLENT MATERIAL TO USE FOR CARVING A MASTER. IT IS EASY TO CARVE INTRICATE DESIGNS INTO WAX AND TO ACHIEVE A SMOOTH FINISH. THE TOOLS OFTEN USED FOR CARVING WAX INCLUDE WAX BLADES, CARVING FILES AND METAL CARVING TOOLS THAT RESEMBLE DENTAL INSTRUMENTS.

The shape of a piece of jewellery can be carved in wax and used to make either a plaster or silicone mould. Carving wax is a smooth, non-brittle wax that can be carved, filed and cut, and it is ideal for carving very detailed designs. There are three grades of wax: green is hard, purple is medium and blue is soft. The softer the wax, the more flexible it is. For pieces with lots of detailed designs, green (hard) wax may be the most appropriate. Carving wax is available as sheets, blocks and ring tubes.

A special wax blade with spiral teeth is inserted into a jewellery saw for cutting wax. Wax files are used for shaping and setting out the general shape, and special carving tools resembling dental instruments are used for more detailed carving. The tips of the tools are heated over a small flame to make carving easier. Once a piece is carved, it is filed with needle files and the surface is finished with

WAX-CARVING TOOLS
From the left; ring sizer with a blade on the edge, wax file, a range of carving tools.

TOOLS AND MATERIALS
CARVING WAX
SCRIBER
JEWELLERY SAW AND WAX BLADE
LARGE WAX FILE
WAX NEEDLE FILES
RING SIZER
WAX-CARVING SET OR A SET OF DENTAL TOOLS
OIL LAMP
SANDPAPER

BASIC WAX CARVING

1 SCRIBING THE DESIGN
Draw your design on the wax using a scriber.

2 CUTTING OUT
Load the wax blade in a jewellery saw (see page 22). Place the blade on the wax and cut around the design. If you are cutting a tube of ring wax, score a line around the wax and cut through the surface, then turn and cut. Continue in the same way until you have cut all the way through. Don't be tempted to cut straight through, as this will result in an uneven shape.

fine sandpaper. It's worth spending time on the finishing because every imperfection will be visible on the finished cast piece. The wax may break during the carving process but can be repaired with a hot carving blade.

CARVING TOOLS

Wax-carving tools are metal tools with a different shaped head on each end. There are several shapes to choose from, including scoop, pointed and flat heads. Along with hand-carving tools, there are some electrical tools used for melting and repairing broken pieces. Wax files are very different from metal files. They have coarse teeth that can remove material very quickly. A set of needle and half-round wax files is a good starting set.

5 USING WAX-CARVING TOOLS

Wax-carving tools that have different-shaped metal tips are used for detailed carving. The tools can be used directly on the wax as they are or the tips can be heated to aid carving.

7 FINISHING

Once the carving is complete, sand the wax with fine sandpaper until all the scratches have been removed. Tear off a small piece of paper to sand hard-to-reach areas. The wax should have a smooth surface. It is now ready to use as a master for a silicone (see page 140) or plaster (see page 143) mould.

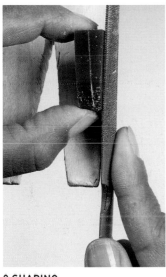

3 SHAPING

Use a large wax file to remove most of the wax and to set out the general shape. Use needle files to carve more detailed shapes and design. If the file becomes clogged, clean it with a wire brush. If you are working with a block of wax, cut out the initial shape with a jewellery saw.

4 USING A RING SIZER

The inside of a ring can be shaped with a ring sizer, which is a tapered tube with a blade on one side. Place the ring sizer inside the hole and press the blade against the wax. The ring sizer should move freely inside the hole. Remove a small amount of wax with each turn. If too much wax is removed at one time, you will have ridges inside the ring.

6 REPAIRING MISTAKES

If you carve away too much wax, heat the tip of a sharp carving tool and use it to scoop up some wax from a spare piece. Allow the melted wax to drip onto the piece; you can then continue carving. This method can also be used to repair a broken area. A sharp tool, such as a blade or pointed tip can be heated and inserted into the broken crack to melt the pieces together. You may need to repeat this a few times until the area is joined. It can then be sanded and finished.

DECORATIVE EFFECTS

THE SURFACE OF A MATERIAL CAN BE MANIPULATED IN MANY DIFFERENT WAYS TO GIVE A DECORATIVE EFFECT. TEXTURES CAN ADD INTEREST TO A PLAIN SURFACE, AND VISUAL EFFECTS CAN ALTER COLOUR, TEXTURE OR SHAPE.

METAL EFFECTS
Different decorative effects can be achieved on metal, using hammers, finishing tools and rolling mills.

KNITTED WIRE
Twenty-two-gauge brass wire was knitted and half-sprayed black.

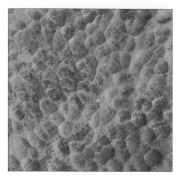

BALL-PEEN HAMMER
Texture made by hammering evenly with the ball end of a ball-peen hammer on copper.

HAMMER: WEDGE END
Pattern produced by hitting the metal with the wedge end of a hammer in parallel lines on copper.

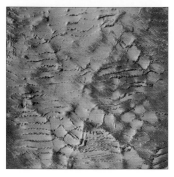

COTTON LACE AND BALL-PEEN HAMMER
Effect achieved by covering annealed metal with cotton lace and using a medium-weight ball-peen hammer to imprint the pattern on copper.

TWISTED LINKS
Lengths of brass wire were twisted and linked together and then sprayed.

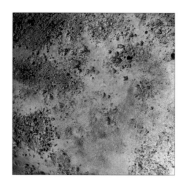

RUSTED HAMMER
An earthy and pit-marked texture achieved by hammering annealed metal with a heavy, rusted hammer.

STEEL WOOL
Matt finish achieved by progressively working through grades 220 to 600 wet-and-dry papers, then applying a moistened, soap-filled, steel-wool pad on silver.

STEEL MOP
The finish was achieved using the polishing machine and a fine stainless steel mop on copper.

PLASTIC AND RUBBER EFFECTS

Plastic and rubber can be manipulated in numerous ways for decorative effects: colour, texture, shape and pattern can all be used in interesting and novel ways.

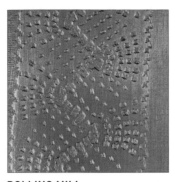

ROLLING MILL: CROCHETED LINEN
Impression made using crocheted linen on copper.

ROLLING MILL: SKELETON LEAF
Impression made using skeleton leaf, highlighted with a black oxide on silver.

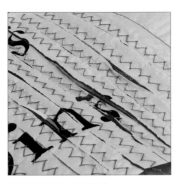

STITCHED BAGS (1)
Plastic shopping bags were layered and stitched with a domestic sewing machine, and slots were cut into the top layer.

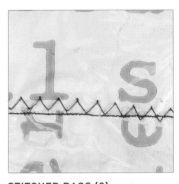

STITCHED BAGS (2)
Plastic shopping bags were layered and stitched with a domestic sewing machine and the edges sealed with a tight zigzag stitch.

ROLLING MILL: PAPER CUT-OUT
Impression made using a pattern cut from watercolour paper on silver.

ROLLING MILL: PERFORATED STEEL SHEET
Impression made using industrial perforated steel sheet on brass.

SCREEN-PRINTED POLYPROPYLENE
A sheet of translucent polypropylene was screen-printed with a pink pattern.

WIRE AND RUBBER
Holes were punched through a sheet of rubber and clear nylon wires were threaded through the holes.

RESIN EFFECTS
The look of resin can be altered by colouring it and by embedding it with other materials.

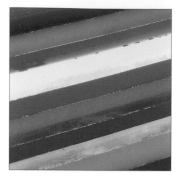

LAMINATED STRIPES
Thin strips of opaque and transparent acrylic sheets were laminated together to form a multicoloured sheet.

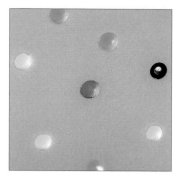

INLAID ACRYLIC
A piece of acrylic sheet was inlaid with acrylic rods. Holes the same diameter as the rods were drilled into the sheet, and the rods were then pressed into the holes and bonded with a liquid solvent.

MARBLED RESIN (1)
Green polyester resin was poured into a mould and allowed to set for two hours, then blue resin was poured over the top. A small amount of yellow resin was poured over the blue mixture, and a thin stick was used to form a marbled effect.

MARBLED RESIN (2)
A mixture of red polyester resin was poured into a mould, and drops of blue resin mixture were placed over the red. The drops blended into the red mixture to create a subtle marbled effect.

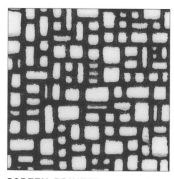

SCREEN-PRINTED POLYSTYRENE
A sheet of white polystyrene was screen printed with a pink pattern.

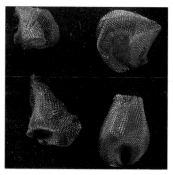

FABRIC AND RUBBER
Holes were punched into a sheet of 2mm (¹⁄₁₆in) thick rubber and a sheet of fabric was pulled through the holes.

EMBEDDED THREADS
Threads were placed in the base of a mould, and a thin layer of clear polyester resin was poured over them. Two hours later a thin layer of red resin was poured over the clear resin to create a red background to the embedded threads.

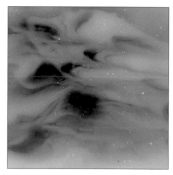

MARBLED RESIN (3)
A mixture of yellow polyester resin was poured into a mould and allowed to set for one hour. Then small amounts of blue resin were poured over, and the two were mixed together.

FABRIC, FIBRE AND LEATHER TEXTURES

Fabric, fibre and leather hold a wealth of possibilities when it comes to decorative effects: stitching, steaming, creasing and layering to name a few.

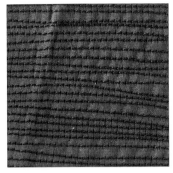

POLYESTER
Several layers of lightweight polyester have been layered and stitched together with cotton thread.

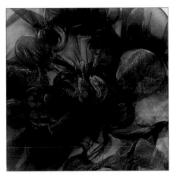

BEAD SHAPES
Beads were wrapped in polyester fabric and tied in with string, then steamed for thirty minutes to give a raised, textured effect.

COLOURED CREASES
The fabric was creased and ironed to make permanent folds, and a heat-sensitive coloured paper was placed over the fabric and ironed again to transfer the colour onto the fabric.

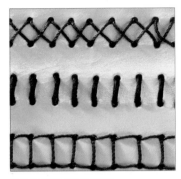

STITCHED LEATHER
Three different types of stitches were created by punching small holes in the leather – a thick leather cord was used to create the pattern.

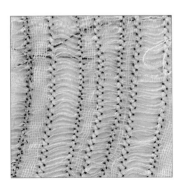

MUSLIN
A piece of muslin fabric was stitched with a zigzag stitch, and the strands between the stitches were removed.

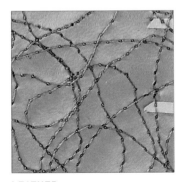

LEATHER
A random series of lines were created on leather using a domestic sewing machine and a needle designed for use on leather.

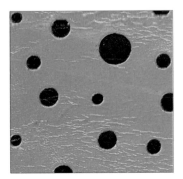

LAYERED LEATHER
Two pieces of leather were layered and glued together with holes punched out of the top piece to reveal the colour of the bottom piece.

FABRIC BUTTONS
These fabric buttons were covered with velvet and tied onto a ribbon to make a necklace.

PAPER AND WOOD EFFECTS

Paper and wood can be combined with other materials, such as wire, acrylic and thread, and printed on for a variety of different effects.

GOLD BALLS
The ends of a thin strip of gold wire were melted to form balls and knotted onto several strands of cotton thread.

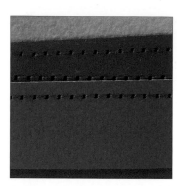

FABRIC AND PAPER LAYERS (1)
Two sheets of paper were layered with lightweight polyester fabric and stitched together.

SCREEN-PRINTED TRACING PAPER
Tracing paper was screen printed, and pieces of newsprint paper were glued onto the surface and then pealed away to leave uneven edges.

THREADS AND TISSUE PAPER
Cotton threads were placed in strips of tissue paper and twisted together.

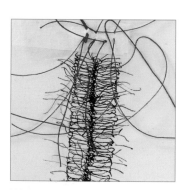

MASKING TAPE
Cotton threads were sewn into a strip of masking tape.

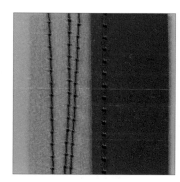

FABRIC AND PAPER LAYERS (2)
One sheet of paper and lightweight polyester fabric were layered and stitched together.

LACE PRINT
A sheet of lace fabric was used to create a pattern on a silk screen and then printed onto paper.

COILED PAPER
Thin strips of paper were coiled and glued onto a paper surface.

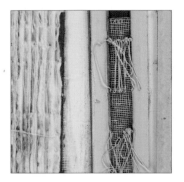

BOOK BINDINGS
The pages of old books
were removed to reveal the
binding threads.

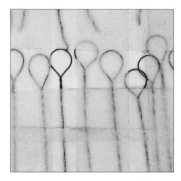

WIRE AND MASKING TAPE
Steel wire was twisted and taped
over with masking tape. As the tape
ages, it becomes more translucent.

STITCHED MASKING TAPE (1)
Two sheets of masking tape were
layered and zigzag stitched, and
holes were cut away from the inside
of some shapes.

PRINTED PLYWOOD
A sheet of plywood was screen
printed with acrylic ink.

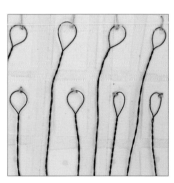

WIRE AND PAPER
Steel wires were twisted and sewn
onto a sheet of paper.

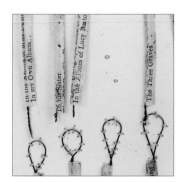

WIRE AND BOOK PAGES
Steel wire was twisted and wrapped
with the pages of an old book.

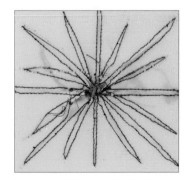

STITCHED MASKING TAPE (2)
Two sheets of masking tape were
layered and stitched with a domestic
sewing machine. Slots were cut
between the stitched marks to add a
three-dimensional effect.

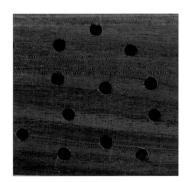

WALNUT AND ACRYLIC
Holes were drilled into walnut wood,
and coloured acrylic rods were
pressed into the holes. (A small
amount of glue can be used to
secure the rods in the holes.)

CLASPS AND CLOSURES

CLASPS AND CLOSURES ARE THE MOST IMPORTANT ASPECT OF A PIECE OF JEWELLERY AND ARE WORTH CONSIDERING IN THE INITIAL DESIGN STAGES. SOME PIECES REQUIRE INGENIOUS SOLUTIONS, ESPECIALLY WHERE DIFFERENT MATERIALS ARE USED TOGETHER. A CLASP MAY BE DISCREET OR USED AS THE MAIN FEATURE AND SHOULD FOLLOW THE AESTHETIC OF A PIECE. THE PRIMARY CONCERNS ARE THAT IT SHOULD BE SECURE AND EASY TO USE.

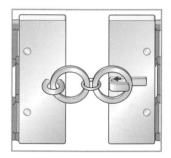

HINGE AND PIN

This bracelet is made of several pieces hinged together. The clasp is hinged and held together with a pin made of tapered wire, attached to the bracelet with a chain for safe-keeping.

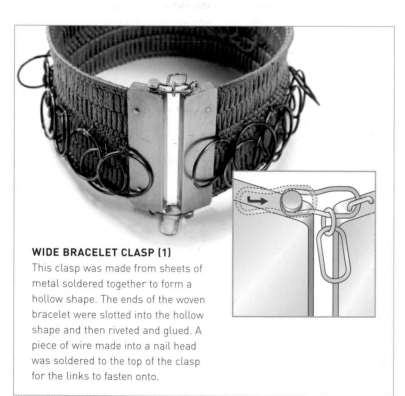

WIDE BRACELET CLASP (1)

This clasp was made from sheets of metal soldered together to form a hollow shape. The ends of the woven bracelet were slotted into the hollow shape and then riveted and glued. A piece of wire made into a nail head was soldered to the top of the clasp for the links to fasten onto.

WIDE BRACELET CLASP (2)

The clasp was made from sheets of silver soldered together to create a hollow form. The ends of the bracelet were slotted into the hollow form and then riveted and glued. A hook was soldered on one side and two linked jump rings were attached to the other side to close the clasp.

HOOK CLASP

A hook clasp is one of the simplest clasps to make. A short, linked chain is attached to one side of the clasp to allow the wearer to adjust the size.

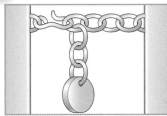

BUTTONED CHOKER

This choker was made with covered buttons sewn onto fabric. A thin strip of metal was sewn into the ends of the fabric. The clasp was made with oxidized silver that had been riveted and glued to the ends. A piece of wire was soldered inside the metal button and a tube with the same size diameter as the wire was soldered on the other side of the clasp. The wire fits inside the tube and is held in place by tension.

U-SHAPED LINK

The clasp was made to look like a chain link, and a small space was left to allow the U-shaped link to slide through.

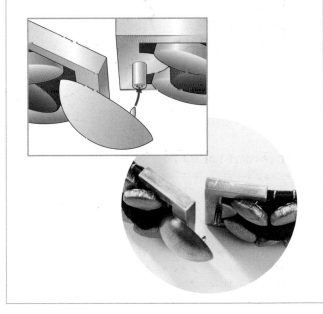

GLOSSARY

ACRYLIC A thermoplastic material that softens when heated. It is available in a wide range of colours, translucent, opaque and clear.

ADHESIVE A sticky substance, such as glue, used for fixing things together.

BEZEL The rim of metal that is used to secure a stone in a rub-over setting.

BINDING WIRE Iron or steel wire used to secure components together during soldering.

BISQUE FIRING This is the name given to the first firing of clay, which makes it more durable for handling but leaves it porous enough to take added colour and glaze.

BORAX A type of flux.

BURNISH To polish by rubbing, usually with a polished steel tool.

BURR Metal tools for grinding, for use with a pendant drill or a flexible shaft motor.

CASTING The pouring of concrete, molten metal, plastic or paper pulp into a mould.

CENTRE PUNCH A pointed punch used to make an indent in metal prior to drilling.

CHUCK The jaws of a drill or a lathe that hold a tool or piece of work.

CONFETTI Paper-thin fragments of glass used to decorate fused-glass jewellery.

COUNTERSINK The enlargement of the entry to a hole.

CURING The process of liquid components turning solid – resin, for example.

DAPPING BLOCK SEE DOMING BLOCK

DAPPING PUNCHES SEE DOMING PUNCHES

DIE Tools used for shaping by stamping, or a cutting tool used for cutting screw threads.

DOMING BLOCK Also Dapping block A steel form with hemispherical depressions used to form domes.

DOMING PUNCHES ALSO DAPPING PUNCHES Steel punches with rounded heads used with a doming block to make domes.

DRAW PLATE A steel tool comprised of a series of tapered holes of diminishing sizes through which wire is pulled to transform its shape.

DYE Powdered substance that changes the colour of items to which it's applied.

EMERY STICK A small wooden stick with emery paper stuck onto it. May be flat or curved.

FINDINGS Commercially made jewellery fittings.

FINISH The cleaning of a piece by sanding and polishing.

FIRESCALE A layer of discoloration on sterling/standard silver that is the result of annealing or soldering.

FIRESTAIN See Firescale

FITTINGS Functional components such as catches, clasps and joints, as used in jewellery.

FLEXSHAFT MOTOR An electrical handheld tool with a flexible cable connecting the tool to the motor. Many different attachments are available, ranging from drill bits to polishing wheels.

FLOCKING A process in which a fabric-like coating of uniform-length nylon fibres is glued to a surface using a special electrostatic flocking machine.

FLUX A chemical used as an antioxidant as part of the soldering process.

FORMER A form, generally made of steel, used to support metal while it is being formed.

FRETWORK A sheet that has been pierced with a number of holes or shapes to make an ornamental pattern.

FUSING GLASS A technique used to make glass jewellery where coloured glass pieces are layered together on a kiln shelf and heated until they fuse together.

GAUGE A standard of measurement, such as the thickness of sheet or the diameter of wire.

GLAZE FIRING Once a clay piece is decorated with underglaze colours it needs to be fired once more, the 'glaze firing'.

HEAT FORMING Shaping acrylic sheets and rods using heat.

INLAY The process of setting one material into another, such as metal into rubber.

JOIN/JOINT The meeting of two or more pieces, often in terms of soldering.

JUMP RING Plain ring forms used in jewellery, not including finger rings.

KEYING Texturing a surface to be glued with a sandpaper to allow better adhering.

LAMINATE Layers of material (such as acrylic) that are sandwiched together.

MALLEABLE A material that can be readily formed or rolled.

MALLET A non-metal-faced hammer, often made from wood, plastic or hide.

MANDREL A tapered steel rod, usually with a circular cross section, used for shaping or stretching rings or bracelets.

MASTER Prototype used to create a mould from which to cast jewellery pieces. Masters can be made from many different materials, including wood and wax.

MOULDS A hollow form into which resin, concrete, paper, plastic or metal can be poured or moulded for casting.

MOP Also Buffing wheel. A fabric wheel used for polishing, usually with a polishing compound applied to it.

NEEDLE FILE Small file, usually used without a wooden handle and available in a wide variety of cross sections and grits.

NOODLES Long thin strips of glass used to decorate fused-glass jewellery.

OVERLAY Welding two pieces of a material together to increase thickness or for decorative effects.

PALLIONS Small pieces of solder.

PATINA A surface finish that develops on metal or other material as a result of exposure to chemicals or handling.

PICKLE A chemical solution used to remove the oxides that are a result of heating.

PIN A piece of wire with a sharpened end used to fasten an object.

PLASTIC Term used to describe a range of synthetic and semi-synthetic products of polymerization: the process of combining molecules through heat or pressure to result in a solid material.

PULP Small pieces of paper mixed with water and used for casting a new sheet of paper.

PUNCHES Hardened steel tools used in forming or texturing metal.

QUENCH Dropping hot metal straight into water for rapid cooling and hardening.

RESIN Resin is liquid plastic that can be cast into any shape.

RING CLAMP A hinged clamp with leather-lined jaws that is tightened either with a wing nut or a wedge.

RIVET Wire or tube used to join two or more pieces when its headless end is hammered.

ROD A straight, solid piece of wire, plastic or rubber.

RUBBER Natural or synthetically produced material, which is soft, smooth and stretchy.

SCREEN PRINTING Process for printing designs onto plastic, paper, or fabric using a mesh screen and specialist inks.

SHANK Straight or plain section of a ring or twist drill bit.

SHEET A piece of metal, plastic or rubber that is normally of uniform thickness.

SKIVING The process of making leather thinner using a special knife.

SOLDER A fusible alloy for joining metals.

SPRUE A passage through which a casting material, for example, resin, can be poured into a mould.

STRINGING Suspending beads, buttons and tassels on beading thread, wire or leather to make necklaces or bracelets.

SWEAT SOLDERING A method of soldering large pieces of metal and long, continuous seams together face to face. The pallions of solder are fused to one or two of the surfaces before the pieces are placed together and reheated to join them.

TEMPLATE A shaped thin plate used as a guide to define a form.

UNDERCUT Areas of a three-dimensional form that have been recessed and may inhibit easy removal from a mould.

UNDERGLAZE COLOUR Commercially available colours that can be bought in powder form or in premixed tubes. They can be painted onto bisque-fired clay pieces.

VACUUM FORMING Process in which a specialist machine is used to heat and stretch sheet plastic over a mould.

WORK-HARDENING The hardening or strengthening of metal by manipulation.

INDEX

CREDITS

Quarto would like to thank the following artists,
who are acknowledged beside their work:

Andre Ribeiro, Angela O'Kelly, Burcu
Buyukunal, Brian Whitewick, Catherine Hills,
Daisy Choi, Elizabeth Olver, Hu Jun, Frieda
Munro, Fritz Maierhofer, Jane Adam, Jane
Willingale, Jennifer Saners, Joanna Gollberg,
Joanne Haywood, Karla Schabert, Kelvin Birk,
Kirsten Bak, Lesley Strickland, Loukia
Richards, Marianne Anderson, Marlene
McKibbin, Melanie Eddy, Melissa Hansom,
Mette Jensen, Min-Ji Cho, Naoko Yoshizawa,
Natalya Pinchuk, Ornella Iannuzzi, Patrizia
Iacino, Philip Sajet, Rachel McKnight, Ralph
Bakker, Ramon Puig Cuyàs, Renee Bevan,
Ruth Tomlinson, Rosie Wolfenden, Sarah King,
Silvina Romero, Tanya Igic, Tina Lilienthal,
Tomasz Donocik, Uli Rapp, Zoe Robertson

DEDICATION

I would like to dedicate this book to my husband,
Alasdair Waugh, for his love, support and wisdom
throughout this project.

Vannetta Seecharran

Author's website: www.vannetta.com